South Portland:

A Nostalgic Look at Our Neighborhood Stores

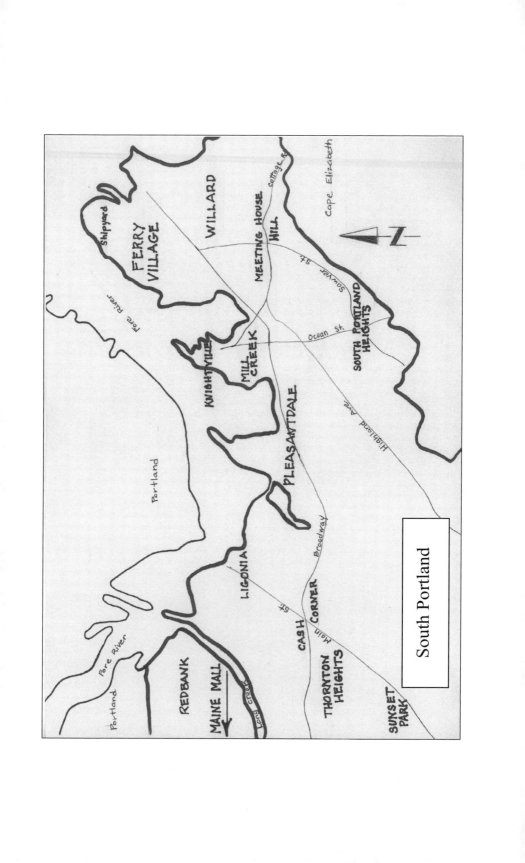

South Portland

South Portland:

A Nostalgic Look at Our Neighborhood Stores

Kathryn Onos DiPhilippo

Barren Hill Books
South Portland, Maine

ISBN 0-9769896-0-3

Cover design by Mason Philip Smith, The Provincial Press
Map illustrations by Edward DiPhilippo
Cover photograph courtesy of John Palanza

Published by:
Barren Hill Books
646 Highland Avenue
South Portland, ME 04106
www.BarrenHillBooks.com
email: info@BarrenHillBooks.com

TABLE OF CONTENTS

Preface

History is all around us, in the places we go and in the people we meet. These connections with both people and places become part of our own personal history. This personal history amasses over our lifetimes, for the most part, entirely in our heads. Unfortunately, when this personal history is not written down, we lose it because our community changes with the passage of time.

Over the course of researching this book, I interviewed hundreds of current and former residents of South Portland. It was interesting that whether I was talking with someone in their 90's or someone in their 30's, everyone had their own childhood memories, whether they were from the 1920s or the 1980s. It was intriguing to find that no matter how many people I spoke with about one particular store, every person had their own unique memories of the store - although most everyone remembered the candy! Different eyes see different things.

This book started out as a bit of an obsession. My childhood in South Portland covered the 1970s and 1980s and my fondest memories are of the L&A Variety store on the corner of Elm and Broadway, and trips to Mill Creek where I would go to King's, Wellwood's, and the Bowl-A-Rama. Anyhow, I wanted to find a picture of King's and Wellwood's, and after searching the various local historical societies and museums and calling multitudes of people who had their own personal photos, no pictures turned up. It occurred to me that if no one thought to take a photo of their corner store, the history of that place would exist only in the minds of the shopkeeper and the store's customers. Thus began my quest to preserve the memory of our neighborhood stores.

This book is definitely not a "complete" history of the stores in South Portland. Thousands of stores have conducted business in our city, many for only a short period of time. Maybe a thousand-page reference book would have done the trick, but obviously I could not include every store in this book. I have tried to include those stores which could be considered South Portland "landmarks", having run for a long period of time, or store locations which have housed multiple businesses over time. My focus was on the past 100 years; however, in some cases if a store was already in existence, I did more research to attempt to identify its year of origin.

That said, there are over 800 stores and shopkeepers identified in this book. To assist the reader in finding information on particular stores, I have used several methods. *First*, a map is located at the start of each chapter. The map illustrations are intended solely to assist the reader in approximate locations; maps are not drawn to scale and do not include all store sites. In some cases, many side streets were left off of the maps to put more focus on those streets which had retail store activity. *Second*, the chapters are set up geographically and in order as if one were traveling down the street. As each building location is described, the first appearance of the address is underlined. *Third*, an index at the end of the book identifies most of the stores. Those stores which are found in the index are also highlighted in bold in the text.

I've had the pleasure of talking to hundreds of people who have lived in South Portland, as well as many who have either themselves run a store in the city, or perhaps had parents or grandparents who did. It has been such a joy reaching out and connecting with these people. It is an honor to record the oral history of our fine city and I am pleased to have documented the story of our many stores and shopkeepers in South Portland.

One final note: if you read through this book and find stores that I have not documented, I would love to hear from you. Perhaps the next time that you look through your family photo albums, you might look in the background of that picture of your sister and see if you have accidentally captured the image of your corner store. Please feel free to contact me and I will continue documenting the history of our neighborhood stores.

I hope you enjoy the book!

K.D.

Introduction

Prior to 1895, South Portland was part of the town of Cape Elizabeth. In those early days, the most populous area of the town was the northern section, which was made up of distinct villages, the larger of those being Ferry Village, Willard and Knightville, where fishing and shipbuilding communities had grown. Although these villages were part of the town of Cape Elizabeth, many had already begun using the South Portland name to differentiate themselves from the southern section, which was largely agricultural. For example, a store on Sawyer Street would list its address as "Sawyer Street, Ferry Village, SP."

In 1895, South Portland split off on its own and, in 1898, became a city. As the 20th century opened, South Portland had begun to move away from its origins as a fishing and shipbuilding community.

The original seven villages that made up South Portland were mostly independent and self-contained, with their own groceries, pharmacies, post offices, schools, churches, barbers, and other providers of goods and services. In the early decades of the 1900s, these "neighborhood shopping centers" were necessary for two primary reasons: goods/services needed to be located close to residential homes, as walking was the most common mode of transportation; and frequent shopping was a must, as homes did not have refrigerators and the household icebox could not keep perishable foods fresh for long.

Shopping in the early 20th century took primarily two forms: some goods could be purchased from the neighborhood grocer, and many goods could be purchased from a deliveryman at the door, such as milk, bread, fruits, meats, ice, coal, and kerosene. Over the past 100 years, there have been a number of major events which have caused substantial changes to the city, its villages, and the way people lived, shopped, and entertained themselves.

One of the first major changes in the shopping habits of South Portland residents was due to the opening of the Million Dollar Bridge on July 20, 1916. The wooden bridge that preceded it was known as the Portland Bridge, which had also come to be known as "The Gridiron of Death". Apparently, the early bridge had gaps large enough for a cow to slip through (and some did!).

Once the Million Dollar Bridge opened, traveling between South Portland and Portland was much easier. The newly-constructed bridge was more conducive to walking across, and people took advantage of that to go to the theater or shop in the stores on Congress Street. As South Portland moved further in the direction of becoming a "bedroom community", more suburban housing came to the city.

Probably the single most dramatic event which changed the look and feel of South Portland was the building of the shipyards during World War II. The East Yard was built in 1940 (in the vicinity of the present-day Breakwater

Condominiums) and not long thereafter, the West Yard followed, close to Front Street in Ferry Village. In addition to the 30 "Ocean" ships built at the East Yard in the beginning of the war, the workers at these two shipyards went on to build 236 "Liberty" ships for the U.S. and its allies throughout the war years.

Two of the enormous ramifications of the shipbuilding effort were the taking of Cushing's Point and the influx of defense workers. A whole section of South Portland, known as Cushing's Point, needed to be cleared to make way for the shipyards. Houses that had belonged to families for generations had to be moved or torn down. As the cove at Cushing's Point was filled, streets disappeared. The whole neighborhood was sacrificed for the war effort.

Then, tens of thousands of shipyard workers, working around the clock in three shifts, descended upon South Portland, and like a wave spread across the city in need of housing and supplies for their families. Housing developments like Redbank Village, Peary Village, and Mountain View sprung up; stores to support the housing followed. Dozens of lunchrooms were established in the Ferry Village area, many operating right out of the homes of local residents, to serve hungry workers on their short food breaks. When a shift let out, the streets of Ferry Village and Willard teemed with cars and people.

In the 1950s and '60s, in cities and towns across America, the advent of the supermarket and the shopping plaza spelled doom for the neighborhood grocer. A way of life changed. In South Portland, each village was its own community, with a grocer, pharmacy, barber, school, and church, within walking distance of residents. When the shopping plaza concept arrived, residents could enjoy a shopping excursion. As more customers headed to the larger stores, neighborhood businesses started to dry up. In South Portland, there had once been A&P stores in Ferry Village, Willard Square, Meeting House Hill, Knightville, Pleasantdale and Thornton Heights, as well as Red & White stores in Redbank, at Cash Corner, in Pleasantdale, near Highland & Evans, and at the top and bottom of Meeting House Hill. These small chain stores, along with other independent stores, eventually closed their doors, unable to compete with the larger one-stop-shopping supermarkets and shopping centers.

The construction of I-295 in the early 1970s, combined with the earlier construction of the Maine Turnpike, had a tremendous impact on the Thornton Heights area. Drivers had previously traveled on Route 1, our Main Street, which had always been the north/south connector along the coast. Now traffic was diverted to the major highway and bypassed the neighborhood stores there.

The Maine Mall area in South Portland now sits as a symbol of the enormous change that has occurred in our shopping habits. From the days of yesteryear when a walk to the neighborhood store was as far as one needed to travel, shoppers today use their cars and computers to purchase the goods they need for everyday life.

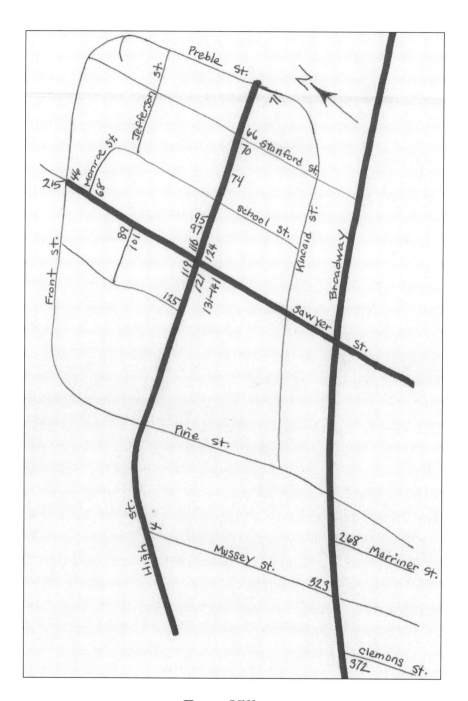

Ferry Village

One

Ferry Village

Ferry Village is one of the original seven "villages" that made up South Portland when the town broke away from Cape Elizabeth in 1895. At that time and well into the 1900s, Ferry Village was the most populous and "well-to-do" neighborhood in the city. Home to several shipyards, sardine factories, a bicycle manufacturing company, and a hardware/equipment manufacturer, Ferry Village offered a wide array of employment opportunities. At one point, there were even four different churches in Ferry Village, all located within about two blocks of each other.

Although early maps of Cape Elizabeth show the Village as encompassing a land area extending all the way to Cottage Road, those who live there have varied opinions on which land truly comprises the neighborhood. Some residents go so far as to define the "true" Ferry Villagers as being those who live on the water side of Kincaid Street.

The "downtown" of Ferry Village is located at the intersection of Sawyer and High Streets. Formerly a one-stop shopping mecca for local residents, over the years the intersection has housed groceries, pharmacies, barbershops, a theater, and a savings and loan.

This circa 1900 Ferry Village photo shows Eben Simonton's barber shop. The barbers in the white coats are Eben Simonton and his son, George.
Angell Glass Plate Negative Collection, Portland Harbor Museum

The photo above was taken circa 1910 and shows Fred C. Gibbs' business at 124 Sawyer, at the corner of High Street. The old Peoples Methodist Episcopal Church can be seen further down on High Street. Gibbs would later move to a location further up High Street and W.W. Rich & Sons would take up residence on this corner.

Courtesy of Belle Graney

The large building at 124 Sawyer has been home to many businesses, including **Clarence Merriman,** grocer, and **Fred C. Gibbs Shoes** in the early 1910s, and the long-running **W.W. Rich & Sons** store, among others.

W.W. Rich & Sons had a long history in Ferry Village, starting out in the 1890s as a livery stable. By the early 1900s, William W. Rich was running a bakery/grocery at 104 Sawyer Street. He opened the store at 124 Sawyer Street in 1914 with his sons, Lewis and Mulford. After William Rich's death in July 1924, his two sons continued to run the business with Mulford as the meat cutter, and Lewis running the grocery.

In the early years of the store's history, there was a soda fountain on the left as you entered, with a counter and high stools. The meat counter was along the back wall with a glass case in front, and customers would come to the counter and give their list of items to a clerk who would then retrieve them. Over the years, the store's layout changed, the soda fountain was eventually replaced by a produce display, and customers could come in and pick out their own items from the shelves. Frank Greenlaw, who used to work at Rich's, remembers, "They had a molasses barrel with a pump on the top, and when customers wanted molasses, I would pump it out into a cardboard container for them."

W.W. Rich & Sons at 124 Sawyer Street

Courtesy of Herbert Pray

In August 1944, Mulford died and Lewis went on to run the business for almost two more decades. After the store closed in the early 1960s, **Haskell's Nation Wide** moved into the building from its former location at 512 Ocean Street. Haskell's operated there through the mid-1970s. Later stores occupying the building include **Schools' Market**, **Kyle's Market**, **The Village Market**, **Village General Store** and **Grandma's Attic** antiques store. **Serenity Hair Care and Day Spa** is now located on the second floor of the building.

Fred Gibbs originally ran a clothing store at 88 High Street, and then moved into the corner of the 124 Sawyer Street building around 1906. This new business, **Fred C. Gibbs' Boots and Shoes**, would run from the busy intersection until around 1913, when Gibbs moved his business to 125 High Street. He ran his business from that corner of High and Dyer Streets for many decades, up until the end of World War II. Locals remember his store at 125 High Street: as you entered, looking to the right there were shoes lined up on shelves built into the wall, with a ladder that slid along the wall so the clerk could go up to retrieve a pair. Many residents also have memories of Mr. Dinsmore, a very pleasant man who worked at the store. Lucian Dinsmore ran a watch repair business from the store from the mid-1920s until the start of WWII.

In 1890, Aurelius V. Cole was running a store at 121 Sawyer Street, known as *A.V. Cole,* selling groceries and provisions from this corner of Sawyer and High. Then, in the 1910s, *Charles H. Kilby* was operating a grocery from 121 Sawyer; this building is the location of Evelyn's Tavern today.

In the early 1900s, the South Portland Co-operative Association grocer was located in the theater building at the corner of High and Sawyer Streets. In the 1910s, the store moved to 130 Sawyer, and by the early 1920s, the store had moved into its final location of 121 Sawyer.

Most locals who remember the store, at 121 Sawyer, refer to it as "Frank Cole's store". Frank Cole did run this store for many years, along with Edwin Cole and Clifford Cole. From early 1900 to about 1938, it was officially known as *South Portland Co-operative Association*. Around 1939 to 1944, the store became *Cole & Walker*, run by Frank Cole and Philip Walker. Then from about 1945 to 1951, Cole and Walker changed the name of their store to *Sawyer Street Market*.

Resident Adelaide Curran remembers the store when it was run by Frank Cole and Philip Walker. Frank Cole worked inside the store and "Phil Walker was the driver. You'd call in an order and Phil would bring it. Phil lived right out back...it was a wood-sided wagon," she says. Curran also remembers the bananas hanging in the store and how the packages were wrapped. "He [Frank Cole] tied everything in string," she says. She remembers how items were wrapped in wax paper, with the string wrapped round and round the package to hold the paper tight.

Resident Carol Campbell remembers that it was a special treat to buy the loose potato chips at the Co-op. A clerk would scoop the chips into a small nickel bag. "They tasted better in the little paper bags," she says.

After the Sawyer Street Market closed in the early 1950s, the store was vacant for a few years and then there were many other businesses there over the years, including *Nutt's Barber Shop*, *Wood's Restaurant*, *Village Laundromat*, *Village Variety Store* and *Bud's Variety*. *Evelyn's Tavern* opened in the late 1970s and is still in operation today.

In the 1920s, three businesses operated from 141 Sawyer Street: *Thomas Lailer*, a blacksmith; *Sawyer Street Garage*; and *Howard Bates Poolroom*.

In this circa 1920 image looking down Sawyer Street towards the water, the Sawyer Street Garage and Howard Bates poolroom can be seen on the left in the flat-roofed building, with a car sitting out front.

Courtesy of Belle Graney

The Sawyer Street Garage was a Hudson and Essex sales and service operation, run by George Robinson. Robinson's daughter, Belle Graney, remembers, "We always had a new car every year. That was when he'd get one car, he called it the 'demonstrator'. My sister said she thinks she was 15 years old before she realized 'demonstrator' wasn't the brand of car. He'd call and say 'I have a new demonstrator, Mother. I'll come up, we'll take a ride'. He'd keep that car until we sold it…there were two models, a two-door and a four-door. It [the garage] burned during the Depression. It was devastating. And people didn't have adequate insurance then."

After the building at 141 Sawyer burned, a new building at 131 Sawyer was constructed. Sawyer Street Garage and Howard Bates Billiards both began operation in the new building in the early 1930s. The Sawyer Street Garage continued in operation until the mid-1930s. Howard Bates Billiards is described as a popular pool hall for people of all ages. During WWII, a game of pool was only 10 cents a game. Many residents recall that Bates would cash checks for the change. Reportedly, there was "never any trouble" in Bates' pool hall; some residents remember that Mr. Bates always sat in the corner, keeping an eye on the goings-on.

Lewis Miller took over the business in the late 1950s, running *Lewis Miller Billiards* for a few years. Later building occupants include *Nutt's Barber Shop*, *Mr. P's Variety Store*, *Caprio's Variety Store* and *Channel Deli*. *Sawyer Street Studios* has occupied the building since 1989.

Before Sawyer Street Studios moved into this building at 131 Sawyer Street in
1989, it had been vacant for two years, but the signs for the Channel Deli were
still painted on the sides and the pizza man was still up on the roof.
                                                    Courtesy of Sawyer Street Studios

At 119 High Street, on the corner of Sawyer and High Streets (*see photo on
next page*), where the basketball court now stands, a large structure once stood.
A theater was located on the 2nd floor, a hardware store on the first floor, and an
Italian sandwich shop on the first floor under the stairs.

The theater on the second floor was occupied by three different operators
over the years: the ***Nordica Theatre*** in the late 1910s, the ***Strand Theatre*** in
the 1920s and early 1930s, and the ***Seville Theatre*** in the late 1930s.

Kids would head down to the theater on Saturday afternoons. There would
be a movie, maybe a comedy, some news, and a serial that would run on a
continuous loop. Patrons could come in at any time and stay as long as they
wanted, watching the movies several times if they desired. The serial would
always end at an exciting spot so watchers would come back the following
Saturday to see what had happened. Resident Marion Burnham even remembers
the piano player who would play along with the movie.

Proco's Italian Shop was located under the stairs to the theater in the
1930s, serving hot dogs, hamburgers and Italian sandwiches. Proco would later
operate his store at 74 High Street, and then 70 High Street, in the 1940s.

C.A. Tilton & Co. had a long history in Ferry Village. In the 1927 South
Portland High School yearbook, C.A. Tilton & Co. advertised as "Tinknockers
since 1865". In the 1871 Atlas of Rural Cumberland County, C.A. Tilton was
listed as a "manufacturer and dealer in stoves, ranges, tin ware, zinc, lead pipe,
pumps, etc. All kinds of repairing promptly and neatly executed."

The Strand Theatre in 1924, with Tilton's Hardware on the first floor.
Collections of Maine Historical Society

C.A. Tilton operated a hardware store on the first floor of the building into the 1930s. In the late 1930s, Tilton & Dewyea plumbers were operating from the building. By World War II, the building was vacant and was later torn down.

At 101 Sawyer Street, on the corner of Harford Court, was a store that went through many changes. According to the 1871 Atlas, ***J.H. & F.H. Harford*** were "dealers in dry goods, groceries, provisions, meal, flour, grain, crockery, glassware, fancy goods, etc.," through both this store and one in Knightville. The Harfords later became publishers of the *Cape Elizabeth Sentinel*, a local newspaper. At the turn of the 20th century, Frederick H. Harford served as South Portland's Judge of Municipal Court, and James H. Harford served as South Portland's tax assessor.

There have been several other stores at 101 Sawyer Street, as well. One of the longer running stores in South Portland, ***Campbell's***, was established by John J. Campbell in the mid-1910s. His son, Walter, took over the operation in the early 1920s.

Like many stores in its day, Campbell's was not a self-service store. Customers would either tell the clerks what they wanted, or hand them a list of items, and the clerk would walk around the store picking out the items. Resident Carol Campbell remembers that as you entered Campbell's, on the right side of the store were the produce shelves with produce baskets sitting on the floor in front of them. Along the back wall was the counter with product bins in front, and all along the left side was a counter. A store clerk behind the counter would turn around and pick items off the shelves that were lined up against the wall.

J.H. & F.H. Harford at 101 Sawyer Street
Courtesy of the South Portland Historical Society

Former resident Kay Greenlaw also remembers going to the store as a child. "The meat counter was on the far right as you went in," she says. "I remember Walter, he was a very nice man." Campbell's carried loose cookies that customers could buy by the pound. Locals remember the molasses cartwheels, the pantry cookies, and the Mary Janes. The cookies were kept in boxes with a glass front and the clerk would scoop them out.

Resident Marion Burnham used to trade at Campbell's. When there was rationing of sugar and other items during World War II, Campbell would really look out for his regular customers; she says that the rationed items were saved for sale only to the regulars.

After Campbell's closed in the late 1950s, **DiBiase Market** operated there until the mid-1970s, and later **Terroni's Market** and **Maudley's Market** occupied the space.

On the other corner of Harford and Sawyer was the long-running Thompson's grocery at 89 Sawyer Street. As far back as 1890, Charles Thompson was running ***C.F. Thompson & Co.*** According to his great-grandson Benjamin Lunt, Charles Thompson later changed the name to C.F. Thompson & Sons when he brought his sons, Benjamin and Charles, into the business.

At the turn of the 20th century, the business became ***Thompson Bros.***, with the two brothers running the business together into the mid-1910s. Around 1916 and 1917, the grocery was just run by ***Benjamin K. Thompson.***

After the Thompson store closed, the building was used only a few times as a storefront over the years. A shoe repair shop was run by Charles Mason in the 1920s. ***Village Market*** was a grocery run by Harry Littlejohn and John R. Miller around 1937 and 1938.

The Cole Bros. Store at 68 Sawyer Street
Angell Glass Plate Negative Collection, Portland Harbor Museum

On the corner of Sawyer and Monroe Streets, at 68 Sawyer Street, the Cole family ran a store for generations. On the 1871 Rural Atlas of Cumberland County, the site shows "***A.V. and R.M. Cole*** store", dealing in provisions, groceries, flour, grain, dry goods, boots, shoes, and general merchandise. Rotheus Cole was an early shopkeeper. At the turn of the 20th century, the store was known as ***Cole Bros.*** with Albert A. Cole and Arthur W. Cole running the grocery. In the 1940s, the grocery was still in operation, then known as "***A.A. Cole's Market***" with Albert's son, Hiram Cole at the helm. Cole's Market closed in the early 1950s.

Cole Bros. delivery wagon in South Portland around 1900
Angell Glass Plate Negative Collection, Portland Harbor Museum

Albion Wilson's drugstore on the corner of Sawyer and Front Street in Ferry Village, around 1899. The small building to the right of Wilson's was occupied by tailor Samuel Harris. The sign hanging out front reads "S. Harris, Ladies & Gents' Tailor".
Angell Glass Plate Negative Collection, Portland Harbor Museum

The building that stands at 46 Sawyer Street today was a drugstore at the turn of the 20th century. ***Albion D. Wilson Druggist***, was in operation for many years. After Albion's death in late 1923, his son Robert took over the store. Robert Wilson ran the drugstore until about 1931 when he moved the pharmacy operation to 171 Front Street. The drugstore remained at 171 Front until the start of World War II when the entire building was moved to 41 Preble Street.

At 46 Sawyer Street, Wilson's Drug Store was similar to many of the early drugstores: in addition to a prescription counter, there was a soda fountain where customers came to get ice cream. The store had black ice cream tables and chairs with wire legs. Resident Marion Burnham remembers that when the girls at the sardine factory were waiting for the boats to come in, Mayor William

McDonald (South Portland mayor from 1920-1925, and later president of the E.W. Brown sardine factory) would take them to Wilson's for an ice cream.

After the drugstore moved out, **Bert D. Spear** operated a grocery from the building around 1932-1933. Around 1935, **Legion Lunch** was operating there, and then the store remained vacant from about 1936 to 1942.

Around 1943, **Bay View Variety Store** opened and ran from 46 Sawyer Street for about 10 years. Around 1954, Bay View Variety moved to another storefront in the same building, 50 Sawyer Street, and continued operating there until about 1960. The storefront at 50 Sawyer had previously been occupied by several barber shops and a fish dealer, as well as two lunchrooms during World War II: the **Marine Grill** around 1943 and **Henry Adams Restaurant** around 1944.

When Bay View Variety switched storefronts, **Myer Jacobson Clothing Store** opened at 46 Sawyer Street, around 1954. Myer Jacobson operated this men's clothing store until his death in September 1963. His widow, Nellie Jacobson continued operating the store into the late 1970s. The building no longer houses any retail stores.

At the foot of Sawyer Street, on the corner of Front and Portland Street, was **Jim's Café** at 215 Front Street. Run by James Paige, Jr., the little café operated here from the mid-1930s to about 1941. Paige then moved his business to 240 Front Street, where he operated from about 1942 to 1943. Local residents refer to the business as "Jimmy Paige's bar room". He sold the business around 1943.

Jim's Café is shown on the left at 215 Front Street. The trolley is turning left from Front Street onto Sawyer. The building corner on the far right in the picture is 46 Sawyer Street.

Collections of Maine Historical Society

Across from the Coast Guard Base, at <u>4 Mussey Street</u>, a small variety store was in existence for several decades, serving primarily the Coast Guard personnel.

Starting back in the mid-1930s, the *Lighthouse Depot* began operation and continued until around 1943. Peter Whitmore and his son, George ran *Whitmore's Variety Store* from about 1944-1946.

Whitmore's was then replaced by *Phil's Variety Store*. Mrs. Emma Aiken, a widow, ran Phil's in the late 1940s. The last operator of a store at that site was Joseph Dies, who operated *Dies Variety Store* in the 1950s. Mr. Dies retired in the late 1950s and the building was demolished.

Courtesy of David Soule

Ginny Whitmore gets a hug from Captain Hodgkins in front of Whitmore's Variety. The store made Italian sandwiches and catered to the Coast Guard base located across the street.

The storefront with the awning is Thurrell's Apothecary at 116 Sawyer Street. Run by pharmacist Albert E. Thurrell, this drugstore was in operation in the 1890s and until around 1917, when Walter Dow took over the business.

Courtesy of Linda Eastman

When Walter Dow first began operating his drugstore at <u>116 Sawyer Street</u>, on the corner of High Street, in the late 1910s, the business was known as **Walter Dow Drugs**. Over the years, the name changed to **Dow's Drug Store**, Russell Newton became proprietor, and around 1952, Paul Kierstead began running the store. Kierstead would later change the store name to **Dow's Sundries**; the store closed in the mid-1960s.

Like other drugstores of its time, Dow's Drugs offered not only prescription medicines, but also a well-loved soda fountain. Resident Cora Shaw Simpson remembers "sitting up on those stools…and they had the best ice cream sodas. Plus, they could mix you up a coke or you could get a cup of coffee." A glass showcase in the store displayed cosmetics and the store sold boxes of chocolates. There were two telephone booths inside and a little post office where you could buy stamps.

Dow's Drug Store at 116 Sawyer Street

Courtesy of Frank and Kay Greenlaw

If you stood on High Street looking at Dow's Drug Store, in a building that used to be located just to the right, there were two stores, side by side. On the left side of the building was 97 High Street, home in the very early days to E.D. Hartcourt, a men and women's clothing store, then A & S Specialty Store in 1920. The site then housed the long-running dry goods store, *Anderson's Variety*.

Norman E. "Allie" Anderson opened the business in the early 1920s and ran it for over four decades; he closed the store around 1963. Allie Anderson sold mostly dry goods: shoes, boots, jackets, underwear, socks, toys, household goods, and thread, among other things. You could even buy fireworks there. Local resident, Cora Shaw Simpson, remembers that going into the store, "on the right as you entered was a glass candy case with the best penny candy. There were hard candies, licorice and caramels. He would put them in a little paper bag to take home."

On the right side of the building was 95 High Street. In the 1910s, *Elmer Cole* ran this very small grocery for a short time, followed by the long-running *A&P*. The original A&P store in Ferry Village was located at 75 High Street for a few years, but by the late 1910s it had moved to 95 High and remained there through World War II. Many local residents remember Sam Klain who ran the store. Former resident, Kay Greenlaw, remembers the old wood floors in the store. Around 1947, a new variety store opened at this site, *Frank's Variety Store*, owned and operated by Frank Richardson.

A few doors down from the old Peoples Methodist Church on High Street, many businesses ran out of the front room of a house that used to stand at 74 High Street. In the early 1900s, *Walter E. Webber* ran a small grocery from the site. Around 1930, the *High Street Market* operated from there, then moved to 70 High Street. In the early 1930s, *Frank Jones* was listed as living and running a bakery business from his home there. In the early 1940s, *High Street Lunch* was operated by Leon Tate, then *Proco's Lunch* opened in the mid-1940s, and then *Janette's Lunch* was opened around 1947 by Janette LaRou. From around 1948 to the mid-1950s, *Larrabee's Restaurant* took over the location. Resident Mike Eastman remembers: "After my grandmother died in 1948, there was no one at home to get me a lunch, so my aunt and father made arrangements with George and Edith Larrabee to have me eat there at noon and they would square up with them at the end of the week. In those days school lunch went from 11:45am-1:15pm. Needless to say, at most it took me 10 minutes to get to the restaurant and another 15 minutes to eat. George didn't want me going back to school too early so would let me play one of the pinball machines. He had a coin on a wire and gave me plenty of games to keep me busy for a while."

On one corner of High and Stanford was 70 High Street, home to the *Blue Bird Stores* from about 1927 to 1931. Blue Bird Stores was a regional grocery chain. After Blue Bird closed, the High Street Market moved here from the building next door and ran until the late 1930s.

After a year's vacancy, the building at 70 High housed ***Everybody's Market*** for a short time around 1940. At the start of World War II, Dominic Proco moved into this space and opened ***Proco's Lunch***. Dominic Proco had previously run the Proco's sandwich shop under the stairs of the Seville Theatre. Resident Herbert Pray remembers the great Italian sandwiches at Proco's. At that time, it was 25 cents for an Italian sandwich.

Towards the end of World War II, Proco moved his lunchroom over to 74 High Street for a short time. The space at 70 High Street remained empty for a few years before ***Jim's Bargain Store*** operated here around 1947. Jim's was a second-hand clothing store. When Dominic Proco came back to this site around 1948, he took over the second-hand store, calling it ***Proco's Bargain Store***. He ran that for a few years, then converted the business to ***Proco's Restaurant*** around 1950. Proco's Restaurant proved to be the last food service establishment at that location. It operated for a short time, then closed. The building remained a residence for some time, but no longer exists today.

On another corner of High and Stanford Street, across from the old Blue Bird Stores building, the Orrs lived in a house at 58 High Street, which served as a rooming house for shipyard workers during the war. In the yard to the side of their house, the Orrs built a small building at 66 High Street and started a grocery, ***Orr's Accomodation Shop***; that shop would run throughout the war years, from roughly 1941 to 1946.

In 1947 and 1948, ***Stevenson's Variety*** was located in the building, run by Edward Stevenson. In 1948, Mrs. Clara Baker took over the store and renamed it ***Baker's Variety Store***; she would run the store through the mid-1950s, when she went up to Broadway and ran the store across from Henley School.

After Baker's Variety left, Violet Pettengill opened ***Violet's Variety Store*** at 66 High Street around 1956. Violet's would be the last store to operate from the little building. By 1960, the store was gone.

At the turn of the 20th century, ***Frank W. Richardson*** was an alderman for the city of South Portland and was operating a grocery at 113 Stanford Street. He would run that store until around 1918.

Around 1919, ***Henry F. Bishop*** was running a fish market from 113 Stanford. By 1920, Ernest E. Webber had opened ***Webber's Cash Market***. In the 1920 program celebrating the city's 25th anniversary, an advertisement for Webber's Cash Market reads "Telephone your order for fancy sea food and choice groceries to Webber's Cash Market...deliveries twice daily at 10 am and 4 pm, successor to H.F. Bishop." Webber's Cash Market closed around 1922 and the building disappears from future directories.

For many years, groceries served the neighborhood from <u>71 Preble Street</u>. There was a store on the first floor with an apartment upstairs. Some of the grocers include the following: *Arthur C. Lailer* – from about 1912 to 1920, and again from 1924 to 1931; *George C. Lailer* – about 1920 to 1923; *John H. Mackin* – mid-1920s; *Kenneth F. Lunt* – early 1930s; *R.M. & R.E. Gott* – around 1933 to 1935; *Crockett's Store* – around 1938 to 1940, moved here from 98 Pickett; and *Ray's Market* – around 1941 to 1942.

Across from the old Henley School, at <u>268 Broadway</u>, a little store served the community for decades. Back around 1917-1918, *Orren H. Randall* ran a small grocery from a house on the corner of Marriner Street. In the early 1920s, the Hamiltons built a separate store on the corner and established *A. J. Hamilton & Son*. That grocery ran until around 1937, then *H.T. Hines & Son* took it over and ran the grocery until about 1940. S. Berton Wilson ran *Wilson's Market* during World War II, and then John Wilson took over and renamed it *Wilson's Store*. Around 1948, Thomas McCready took over Wilson's Store and the store remained in business into the early 1950s.

The variety store across from Henley School can be seen on the left.
Courtesy of South Portland Historical Society

Leeman's Variety Store was in operation from about 1953 to 1955, and then Clara Baker opened *Baker's Variety Store* (Clara Baker had previously operated her store from 66 High Street). Around 1960, Mrs. Edith Larrabee took over the store and renamed it *Larrabee's Variety Store* (Edith Larrabee had previously run a restaurant at 74 High Street). She operated the store for about a decade. The last to do business from the site, *Six to Six Variety Store*, operated in the early 1970s. The building was demolished around 1972.

At 323 Broadway, the original Broadway Market was open for over 50 years. **Broadway Market** began operation back in the early 1930s, run by George E. Haggett; he had previously operated stores at 333 Cottage Road and 185 Preble Street. Edward McGonagle bought the business from Haggett around 1943 and ran it until the late 1950s, when Desmond Bragdon took over the operation. Peter Zaimes bought the business around 1960. Zaimes ran Broadway Market until around 1975 when he sold it to Rose Griffin.

While Rose Griffin ran the market, she was raising three children on her own. This certainly didn't hold her back: she even expanded the business. On the right side of the building was an apartment, later an arcade, then an ice cream shop, an office and a kitchen area. She offered take-out and catering service. According to Rose Griffin's daughter, Joanne, the food was terrific. Rose would make her own meatballs and sauce. "She made the best Italian sandwiches in town," says Joanne. The sandwiches were made with the best ingredients and some of the favorites were the fish sandwich and melted cheese on tuna.

The store later was renamed the **Broadway Deli**, then **Bodge's Broadway Market,** and now **Anania's**.

In October 1941, pharmacist Elmer Anderson applied for a permit to construct a drugstore on the corner of Clemons Street, at 372 Broadway. When the building was completed, he moved his family into the apartment upstairs and went on to run **Anderson's Pharmacy** on the first floor throughout the 1940s and 1950s. The pharmacy sold prescriptions, general items, and had a fountain area. **Hider's Variety** was in operation in that building in the 1960s; that store was run by brothers, Samuel and William Hider. The Hiders had previously operated Capitol Grocery in Thornton Heights. In one of the most tragic incidents in the history of South Portland's stores, in 1969 there was a robbery attempt at Hider's Variety and Samuel Hider was killed. The store closed and the building has been used as apartments ever since.

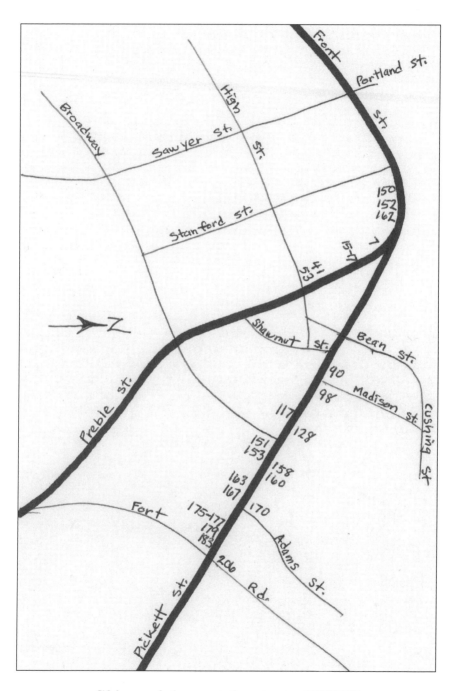

Shipyard Area at the start of WWII

Two

Shipyard Area

Ferry Village, always one of the most populated neighborhoods in South Portland, was bursting with activity during the "Shipyard Years" of World War II. The streets were jammed with cars, the sidewalks were teeming with pedestrians, and there was so little housing available for workers that some people slept in cars in driveways.

There was non-stop activity in the yards. Working in three shifts, the shipyard workers kept the production going at high speed. During shift changes and lunch breaks, the activity spilled out into the surrounding neighborhoods. Many lunchrooms sprung up during that period to feed the thousands of shipyard workers. By the end of the war, most of the lunchrooms closed and never again operated as food service establishments.

Unidentified store serving shipyard workers circa 1941. The house on the left was on the corner of Bean and Cushing Streets. These structures were either moved or torn down to make way for the expanding shipyard.
Courtesy of the South Portland Historical Society

Opposite the main gate to the West Yard, the **So Big Restaurant** at 152 Front Street served shipyard workers during the War. Kay Greenlaw, who worked there when she was a freshman in high school, sold cigarettes and candy behind the counter while her mother cooked hamburgers and hot dogs on the grill. She remembers that even though there were a few tables, most workers would just order their food to take with them. "Those men coming out of that shipyard were hungry," she says.

There were three doors at the front of the building. On the front wall facing the street, there were two cooking areas, each flanked by counters on two sides. There was a grill and one or two steamers at each cooking station, and a window over the grill that opened, to allow customers to be served outside as well. A kitchen and storeroom were located towards the back, with another sales counter for items like cigarettes, chips, whoopie pies and candy.

Evelyn Moran worked in the restaurant and remembers it well: "We sold cigarettes at the grills along with hamburgers and hotdogs…People stood on all sides of us during the 'blows' [lunch breaks were announced by the 'blow' of the steam whistle]. The first time a person was put on the grill to work, he/she was put in as an extra. It took a few seconds to get over the shock of being surrounded by people, all wanting to be waited on at once. Customers were all nice. They waited patiently for their turn."

Employees at the So Big Restaurant on Front Street
Courtesy of Frank and Kay Greenlaw

Carl Lorenzo and Joe Gray ran the So Big. Kay Greenlaw remembers that Joe Gray also ran a small peanut stand next door. Greenlaw would bag the peanuts in little penny bags at the So Big Restaurant, and would take them over to Joe to sell under his umbrella at the stand.

At 150 Front Street, there were several businesses. William Faulkner ran *Bill's Store*, a clothing store, during the war. There were also two small lunchrooms: *Dixie's Lunch*, run by Asa Todd, and *Mike's Lunch*, run by Michael Ferejohn. Later during the war, Mike's Lunch was taken over by Joe

Gray and the name changed to ***Joe's Lunch***. The lunchrooms also sold hamburgers and hot dogs, like the So Big, but on a smaller scale.

Morrison's Restaurant was on the far side of the So Big, farther away from the main gate, at 162 Front Street. That lunchroom was run by Frank Morrison during the war.

Ted's Quick Lunch was just around the corner at 7 Preble Street. In 1941, restauranteur/chef Theodore "Teddy" Hassapelis started selling sandwiches to workers at the main gate to the West Yard on Front Street. At first, he stocked his van with sandwiches that his wife would make in their home in Portland. Hassapelis would drive the van to the West Gate for the workers' break and sell all of the sandwiches. When they were gone, he'd drive back to the house to restock the van. "It was a 24-hour, two person operation," says Hassapelis' son, Peter. With three shifts to serve, Hassapelis would take catnaps between lunch breaks. He quickly earned enough to buy a pull-behind trailer with a little grill inside. Then, within six months of his first sales, he bought the house at 7 Preble Street across from the main gate.

The truck to the right of the building is Teddy Hassapelis' first delivery vehicle. His pull-behind trailer can be seen set up in front of the small building. The tall house to the left is 7 Preble Street which Hassapelis bought and then set up his lunchroom in. Over the years, he would make a number of additions and expansions to the building.

Courtesy of Peter Hassapelis

Hassapelis turned the house into a huge cafeteria. According to Ted's son, Peter Hassapelis, "People would walk all over each other...lunch time was short and so many people needed to eat."

Theodore Hassapelis

Photos courtesy of Peter Hassapelis

Ted's Quick Lunch at 7 Preble Street

The business closed in 1945 when the yard closed. After the war, Hassapelis retired for three years and traveled the United States with his family. In 1949, he started using the building again to manufacture his own "Chef's Brand" mayonnaise. When the Korean War started, there was a jar shortage; when he couldn't get enough jars, he closed the business.

Hassapelis later went on to run other successful restaurants. His son, Peter says, "He was always looking for something new to get into." Teddy Hassapelis was quite a savvy businessman. Peter Hassapelis says that he acquired a new appreciation for his father's gifts when he was taking classes for a business degree. Peter says that when he was learning how to select a business location, he had a strong recollection of sitting with his father in the car when he was young; his father would sit and study the people's movements, and the traffic patterns, intuitively knowing how to pick the right site for a successful business.

The sandwich board on the inside of Ted's Quick Lunch listed cheese sandwiches for 10 cents, ham sandwiches and hamburgers for 15 cents, BLTs for 25 cents, and a whopping 30 cents for a turkey or chicken sandwich.

Courtesy of Peter Hassapelis

Leed's Lunch was located at 15-17 Preble Street during the war. The lunchroom was operated by James J. Leed.

Robert Wilson had previously operated his drugstore at 171 Front Street. Just before WWII, he had the building moved to this site at 41 Preble Street, where he ran ***Wilson Drug Store*** throughout the war. After the war, the drugstore became ***Wilson Variety Store***, operated by Florence Loud in the late 1940s.

At 53 Preble Street, ***The Ship Galley Restaurant*** was in operation during the war. The restaurant was situated on the corner of Preble and High Streets, in the former Knights of Pythias hall.

Resident Adelaide Curran lived on <u>Stanford Street</u> during the war. Across the street from her house, there had been a cornfield which was made into a parking lot for the shipyard workers. Curran remembers **Mrs. Steen's Snack Stand** that was set up in the parking lot. Customers could go to the window and buy soda, cigarettes and snack foods like peanut butter crackers, candy bars and potato chips. On the corner of Stanford and Jefferson Street, the Steens also ran a lodginghouse and **Steen's Restaurant** during the war.

Ralph's Café was established in 1941 at <u>90 Pickett Street</u> by Ralph Mangino; like many other locals, Mangino had converted an existing house into a lunchroom to serve the shipyard workers. As with most homes and businesses on Pickett Street north of Broadway, it was removed when the West Yard was constructed. Mangino would go on to run a store at 108 Broadway, **Rose's Handy Store.** That store was open from 1942 until around the end of WWII.

The store at <u>98 Pickett Street</u>, at the corner of Pickett and Madison Streets, had a long history up until World War II. There were living quarters in the back of the house, with the store located in the front. For several years before and after 1910, **William Johnson** and his wife ran the store. In the early 1910s **Lesser H. Mills** ran it. In the mid-1910s, **Clinton Wendley** ran a grocery there; Wendley then moved his grocery business to 427 Preble Street, in Willard Square. In the mid-1920s, **Byron Peters** proceeded to run the grocery at Pickett and Madison, before turning the operation over to **Stearns & Co.** in the late 1920s.

William Crockett bought the grocery business from Stearns in 1929. Crockett's daughter, Helen Crockett Romano, remembers when her father bought the business. She had long dreamed of running her own store. Around 1930, Herbert Arey took over the store for a year or two, but then the Crocketts took the store back and ran it until the late 1930s. According to Mrs. Romano, Crockett's Store carried the usual variety store fare: groceries, milk, cigarettes and penny candy, and they even ground their own hamburg. Resident Cora Shaw Simpson remembers the smell of the potato chips in the store; you could buy a nickel bag of chips there, too. She also remembers the Coca Cola case and the birch beer.

Helen and her husband, Ray Romano, went on to run Ray's Market at 71 Preble Street for a number of years. However, with Ray working as a welding instructor at the shipyard, and Helen with a new baby to take care of, they decided to give up the store.

After the Crocketts moved their store operation out of 98 Pickett Street, **Levi Miller** ran the grocery in the early 1940s. The last grocer listed at that address was **Ronald E. Lavigne**; when the shipyard took over that portion of Pickett Street, Lavigne moved his grocery business to 54 Broadway.

George J. Ganem opened a diner at 117 Pickett Street in 1941 to serve the workers at the East Yard. According to his brother, John Ganem, the diner was known as ***Ginger & Shirley's,*** and served the typical fast food and sandwiches. When the land was taken over for construction of the West Yard, George Ganem moved his diner to Cash Corner.

At 128 Pickett Street, ***Munson's Lunch Room*** opened in 1941. Established by Fred F. Munson to serve the workers at the East Yard as they built ships for Britain, that restaurant closed in 1942 when the land was needed to be cleared for the expansion of the shipyard. Munson moved the building to 14 Webster Street in the summer of 1942 and operated Munson's Lunch Room at that site until the end of the War.

On Pickett Street, between Broadway and Fort Road, a variety of food establishments opened both in the first wave of shipbuilding, when the East Yard was in production, as well as after the West Yard began operation.

At 151 Pickett Street, ***Mike Nichols*** operated a restaurant in 1941. The ***Casco Grill*** began operation and was open through the remainder of the war.

Mike's Hot Dog Stand, at 153 Pickett Street, was established by Mike Nichols around 1944. Like the others, it closed at the end of the war.

Wallace Proctor erected a building at 158 Pickett Street in 1941 and opened ***Proctor's Lunch***. The lunchroom closed for a short time and the owners of Casco Grill reopened the location as ***Little Casco Restaurant*** around 1943. Around 1945, Harry Littlejohn took over the restaurant business, but he closed it in 1946. The building has been occupied in recent years by the well-received bakery, ***One Fifty Ate.***

Joe's Torpedo Sandwich Station, at 160 Pickett Street, was run by Joseph Cremo around 1944 and 1945. According to his daughter, Mary Rush, the place was just a tiny building with a window. They would make Italian sandwiches at their house and Joe would bring them here to sell to the shipyard workers. The menu was limited: Italian sandwiches, bagged peanuts and soda.

Another home on Pickett Street was converted during WWII. In late 1941, Stella Pearce had a garage demolished on her property at 163 Pickett Street and in March 1942, she applied for a permit to build an addition onto the house for a restaurant. ***Mrs. Stella M. Pearce Lodginghouse & Restaurant*** was established. Toward the end of the war, ***Pearce's Restaurant*** was being run at the site by Arthur Soyias and Sam Davis. When the shipyard shut down, the restaurant closed.

At 167 Pickett Street, ***Thomas J. Rushia*** operated a snack stand from this corner of a large parking lot at 165 Pickett Street.

John Patrinelis ran *Pat's Lunch* from a house at 170 Pickett Street; he also ran *Pat's Diner* around the corner at 1 Adams Street. Although he closed Pat's Diner after the War, he kept Pat's Lunch open for a few more years on Pickett Street. After closing the lunchroom around 1948, he left the store vacant but continued living in the house. Around 1954, he opened Pat's Diner again for a short time, from this 170 Pickett location.

Also on Adams Street, Wilbur D. Faulkner ran both *Bill's Lunch* and *Bill's Working Men's Store* from a building at 3 Adams Street, selling clothing to the shipyard workers. Arthur Schreiber erected a small variety store at 15 Adams Street, known as *Simco Trading Co.*

The *Todd View Restaurant* opened at 177 Pickett Street during WWII. The site proved to be one of the few businesses to survive the closing of the shipyards. It benefited from its location; with Fort Preble and later SMVTI (now SMCC) close by, the little restaurant had another customer base to turn to after the war. The Todd View continued operating through the 1950s and into the early 1960s.

Frank and Lena Federico opened *Federico's Spaghetti House* at the site in the early 1960s. The restaurant continued operating until the building was destroyed by fire and demolished in 1979. Federico then built a new restaurant at 175 Pickett Street. He received a license to operate in May 1980, but by October that same year, the restaurant changed hands and became *Spring Point Café*. The Spring Point Café operated from the site for about 15 years, with several different owner/operators. The restaurant/bar closed in the mid-1990s, until *O'Rourke's Landing* opened for business in 1997.

At 179 Pickett Street, Ruth Higgins ran *Ruth's Sandwich Shop* during the war.

Handy Lunch, at 183 Pickett Street, was established by Elmer Libby in 1941. Libby kept the lunchroom open round-the-clock, seven days a week, serving the shipyard workers. "My dad used to sleep in the car," remembers his son, Elmer. "He probably only closed about three hours during the night to clean," and then opened up again for the next shift.

Although there was a counter inside with a few places to sit and eat, most would order through the front window, eat quickly, and head back to work. The lunchroom served hamburgers, steamed hot dogs, fried clams, and clam cakes. A hot dog and soda combo cost only 17 cents; fried clams were 35 cents a pint or 75 cents a quart.

Handy Lunch closed in 1945, along with most of the other lunchrooms in the area.

Elm Tree Lunch, corner of Pickett Street and Fort Road

Courtesy of Robert Chenevert

Elm Tree Lunch, at <u>206 Pickett Street</u>, was run by Clarence Jacobson from about 1942 to 1946. The photo above was taken a few years after the store had closed; the words "potato chips" can still be seen on the roof facing the shipyard. On the right side of the photo, one of the Fort Preble buildings can be seen in the distance.

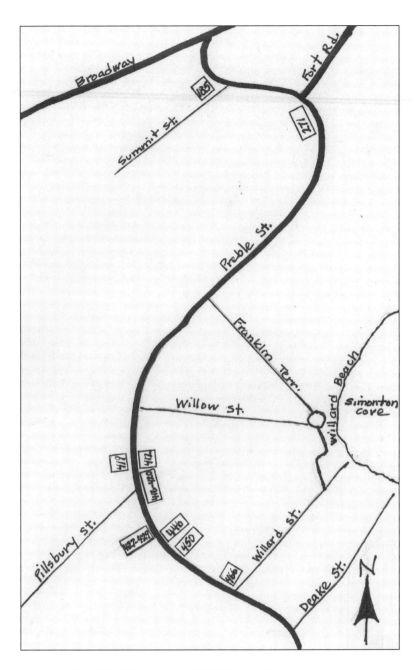

Preble Street and Willard Square area

Three

Willard

In the 1800s, the area around the intersection of Preble and Pillsbury Streets was known as Point Village. By the time South Portland broke away from Cape Elizabeth in 1895, the village had become known as "Willard". The neighborhood was home to many families of fishermen and ship captains, families with names like Loveitt, Woodbury, Angell, Pillsbury and Willard.

Coming up Preble Street from the Ferry Village area, one of the early stores was located at 111 Preble Street, in what was called "Temperance Hall". On the 1871 atlas, *W.J. Royer and D.W. Kincaid* were listed as "dealers in dry goods, groceries, provisions, meal, flour, boots, shoes, crockery ware, glass ware, and general merchandise" at that site. In the early 1900s, *Walter Royer* was listed as running the store, and around 1908, *James C. Desmond* was running a grocery there.

Just across the street, at 112 Preble, *Leavitt J. Colbeth* operated a small grocery in the 1930s. Colbeth had previously operated a store in Ferry Village at 104 Sawyer Street.

Another early store in the area was *Alfred Thrasher & Son* at 185 Preble Street. That store began operation in the mid-1880s on the corner of Summit and Preble Streets, selling groceries and provisions. The building was both a home and a store. Alfred Thrasher and his son, Alfred Jr., ran that store at 185 Preble Street into the early 1900s. From that point forward, there were many different store operators at that site:

Mr. and Mrs. Charles L. Bennett – early 1900s;

Fred E. Anderson – from about 1906 to the mid-1920s. He ran the store with his son, George;

Frank J. Seeley – around 1927. Seeley had previously run a store across from Whitehall in the Pleasantdale section of South Portland;

George E. Haggett – late 1920s. Haggett had previously run a store on Meeting House Hill at 333 Cottage Road. He would go on to run Broadway Market at 323 Broadway in the 1930s and early 1940s;

George H. Anderson – about 1930 to 1932. Fred Anderson's son;

Golden Rule Market – approximately 1932;

Herbert M. Arey – around 1933. Arey had run a store at 219 Preble Street (around 1917-1918), then at 98 Pickett Street before coming to 185 Preble. He later ran a store at 221 Preble Street in the mid-1930s;

Everett L. Inness – from the mid-1930s to about 1946. Resident Herbert Pray remembers that Mr. and Mrs. Inness ran the store and lived upstairs. All the staples were available: canned goods, bread, meats and other groceries. Much of the food was stored in barrels, like sugar and molasses, then measured out for the customer. Mr. and Mrs. Inness ran this store throughout World War II when rationing was in effect;

Deakin's Market – late 1940s. Frederick H. Deakin bought the business after World War II. Resident Herbert Pray remembers that, like other stores of the times, Deakin's Market had switched over from the old barrel-type method of selling food and now carried more pre-packaged food on shelves;

Smith's Market – early-to-mid-1950s, run by Norman and Pearl Smith;

Dick's Meats & Specialities – around 1957. The building still stands at 185 Preble, but has been converted to apartments.

A little further down Preble Street was a grocery at <u>221 Preble Street</u>, run first by **Herbert M. Arey** in the mid-1930s, then by **Dorothy C. Forgione** in the late 1930s.

At 271 Preble Street, **William Griffin** opened a grocery in the mid-1920s. According to Herbert Pray, William Griffin's son, Henry ran the business. Henry's daughter, Leola "used to dip out ice cream for the kids," says Pray. Griffin's store ran until about 1933, then a series of markets ran from the space:

Philip R. Burrowes, *grocer* – about 1934-1935;

Dana A. Wiley, *grocer* – about 1936-1948;

Arthur P. Bonvie, *grocer* – about 1949-1952. After Bonvie's death in 1952, his wife Marion Bonvie continued operating the store, but the store name officially changed at this time to:

Preble Street Cash Market – Mrs. Bonvie first started operating this on her own in 1953. By 1957, Mrs. Rachel Naples was running the store, living in the back. Around 1958, Vincent and Mary Frallicciardi began running the store. According to Rocco Frallicciardi, his parents extended the store throughout the whole first floor. They sold pizza, Italian sandwiches and side dishes. At this time, Southern Maine Vocational Technical Institute had opened and the store received a lot of business from the college students;

Alfonso's Pizza – around 1962, the DePaolo family took over the business and ran first Alfonso's Pizza through the 1970s, then Alfonso's Variety in the 1980s. The store was not in operation in the early 1990s, but in the mid-1990s Alfonso's Market was open once again. The store closed in the late 1990s.

Aroma's – in the early 2000s. Aroma's now operates from 340 Main Street.

271 Preble Street in 1992

Courtesy of the City of South Portland

Willard Square

Over the past century, the intersection of Preble and Pillsbury Streets has been known as Willard Square. At the turn of the century, the trolley line ran through the square carrying visitors to Willard Beach, the Willard Casino and on to Cape Cottage.

During its heyday, the square was teeming with grocery stores, a pharmacy, a post office, a pool room, barber shops and beauty shops. Many residents tell stories of the bonfires that the locals built in the middle of Willard Square to celebrate a win by a South Portland sports team.

During World War II, a scene played out in Willard Square unlike anything that can be imagined today. When the shifts would let out at the shipyards, workers poured into the surrounding area and Willard Square was filled with cars and pedestrians.

In the image above from 1923, the building to the right of the trolley is 416-420 Preble Street, occupied by Leroy M. York Druggist and the A&P store. On the left, in back of the horse watering fountain is the Willard Square Barber Shop at 419 Preble, run by George Simonton.

Courtesy of the South Portland Historical Society

Howard S. Thompson was an early grocer at 412 Preble Street; he ran the IGA store there in the 1920s. The **Willard Square Market/IGA Store** began operation in the 1930s. One of the first proprietors was Winfield E. Darling.

Darling ran the store in Willard Square in the early-to-mid-1930s. Then he sold the business and opened a new store at 59 Angell Avenue, then moved his grocery to 464 Cottage Road.

After Winfield Darling, Arthur E. Jones was the proprietor briefly, but by 1940, Mr. Orman C. "O.C." Cleaves had taken over the operation. He ran the store at 412 Preble with his wife, Abigail. The store was renamed *Cleaves Market* in the late 1940s.

Resident Lois Doyle used to work in Cleaves Market in the 1940s. She says that in the early days, the store was full service, with customers ordering what they wanted at the counter. The store changed over to self-service while she was working there. Cleaves Market was a sizeable store, with four full-time employees. In addition to the usual groceries, the store had a meat counter, a walk-in cooler and a produce display. Like Richardson's next door, Cleaves did not sell beer; the shipyard workers in Willard Square headed over to F.K. Richards to buy that.

In October 1954, George and Christina Bathras bought Cleaves Market. Although for a few years they kept the name and signs for "Cleaves Market", they later changed the name to *Bathras Market.*

Bathras Market in Willard Square   *Courtesy of Christina Bathras*

George and Christina Bathras, or "Mr. and Mrs. B" as they would come to be called, were much loved shopkeepers in Willard Square, looking out for the many children who would stop in the store on their way to and from school. According to Lisa Bathras Flocatoulas, her parents worked long hours with no vacations. "Their work was their lifestyle and they enjoyed immensely seeing the customers and their children/grandchildren and great-grandchildren, who would come back to visit and say 'hello'." She comments on one of the keys to success for a Mom and Pop store, "Before the credit card became the norm, families would run a tab for groceries and pay weekly/bi-weekly. This 35-year practice/service of offering free credit…was a trademark of our store and many others. Customer service and satisfaction were important and essential."

Bathras Market offered a large selection of items, including fresh meats, fish, deli items, produce and groceries, as well as made-to-order Italian sandwiches, beer and wine.

George and Christina Bathras' daughter, Lisa in front of the store.

Photos courtesy of Christina Bathras

When the store eventually closed in 1989, Lisa says her "folks insisted waiting until after Halloween, when all the kids, near and far, came by trick-or-treating. A tradition they looked forward to each year: children with their folks and friends coming in homemade, super costumes, some truly works of art, to visit Mr. and Mrs. 'B' and chat."

George Bathras inside the store with his grandson.

Leroy York ran the drugstore in Willard Square at <u>416 Preble Street</u>, from the early-to-mid-1920s. For most of its drugstore years, the site was also home to Post Office Sub Station No. 10. Ernest L. Nichols took over the drugstore in the mid-1920s.

The ***E.L. Nichols Druggist*** store carried the usual prescriptions and pharmacy sundries. Willard Square resident Herbert Pray remembers being able to get an ice cream cone at the pharmacy. There was a freezer case with a cover that lifted up; inside were popsicles, ice cream bars, and ice cream with brands like Deering, Hood and Fro-Joy.

Willard Square in the mid-1930s, home to the Willard Square (IGA) Market, E.L. Nichols Druggist, and the A&P.   *Courtesy of Christina Bathras*

Around 1938, the E.L. Nichols name was changed to ***Willard Square Pharmacy.*** Willard Square Pharmacy was managed by Roy Woodside, then Donald Calderwood, and finally Austin Bean. Bean changed the name of the pharmacy to ***Austin C. Bean Drugs*** around 1942.

Austin Bean's drugstore at 416 Preble Street was typical of the time period. Prescriptions, magazines, newspapers, cameras, and many other items were offered. There was also a soda fountain on the right side of the store. Resident Barbara Hawkes remembers going to Bean's where "we'd get an ice cream cone for a nickel, or a double decker for a dime." The post office sub station was in the back of the store on the right side. To the left of that was a lending library with all the best-sellers. Former resident David Rice remembers being able to borrow a book for three days for a nickel; there was no city library in those days.

Bean's closed in the late 1950s. Frederick C. Call is listed as the drugstore operator in 1959. The pharmacy was vacated by 1960 and was later occupied by

Caron & Waltz plumbing and heating. The storefront is now home to ***One Fifty Ate*** at Willard Square.

At <u>420 Preble Street</u>, ***The Great Atlantic & Pacific Tea Co. (A&P)*** store was in operation in the 1920s and 1930s. Resident Mildred DeMass remembers it as an old store with sawdust on the floor and a pickle barrel. Many residents fondly remember the original A&P coffee brands in their packages: Eight O'Clock coffee in the red, Bokar in the black, and Red Circle in the yellow.

Around 1941, Fred W. Richardson moved his ***Richardson's Market*** into this store from across the street. Many residents remember Mr. and Mrs. Richardson as very sincere and devout people who did not like drinking and smoking and refused to sell beer or cigarettes in their store. Resident Mildred DeMass recalls, "They ran a beautiful store, cleaned up the floors, they kept that store immaculate…they ground hamburg in front of you, they waited on you entirely…they always had penny candy. If your parents paid their bill, they'd give you a lollipop."

Resident Sylvia Angell remembers looking over the meats at the meat counter and Mr. Richardson commenting, "When in doubt, buy hamburg".

Willard Square in November 1964 was changed considerably. Caron & Waltz had taken over the building formerly occupied by a drugstore and grocery. Bathras Market was now operating at 412 Preble Street. Larry's Variety had begun operating from 419 Preble on the left.

Courtesy of the Portland Press Herald

The ***Willard Square Barber Shop*** was located at <u>419 Preble Street</u>. George Simonton ran that barber shop, and pool room, from the mid-1910s to the early 1930s. Raymond McGeoch ran the pool room for just one year, and Francis K. Richards opened a variety store at the site in the early 1930s, known simply as ***F.K. Richards***. Richards ran the store until his death in 1949. Unlike the stores across the street during the war, F.K. Richards sold beer, cigarettes, and tobacco, and also had darts and a pool room, which made this establishment quite popular with the shipyard workers.

Behind the fire truck is the F.K. Richards store at 419 Preble Street.
Courtesy of the South Portland Historical Society

The F.K. Richards store.   *Courtesy of Sylvia Angell*

Lucien Dumont in the doorway of his store at 419 Preble Street.
Courtesy of Phyllis Dumont

Willard Square Variety was established around 1950 by Lucien and Phyllis Dumont. Lucien Dumont had previously been employed by Francis Richards at the same location. After Mr. Richards died, Dumont purchased the business and changed the store name.

Willard Square Variety carried the standard variety store fare of milk, bread, canned goods, candy, and beer, along with freshly-made Italian sandwiches. There was also a soda fountain in the store. When the pharmacy across the street gave up the post office substation No. 10, the Dumonts took on that operation in their store as well.

Lucien and Phyllis Dumont sold the store in 1963 to Lawrence McGinnis. Mr. McGinnis renamed the store ***Larry's Variety*** and ran the store through the remainder of the 1960s and into the early 1970s.

Willard Square at the turn of the century, S.G. Willard store was in the building.   *Courtesy of Syvia Angell*

Henry Griffin worked at his father-in-law's store at 427 Preble Street. He is seen here with his wife, Isabelle Cobb Griffin, in 1914.

Courtesy of the Henry Griffin family

The building at <u>427-429 Preble Street</u> has a long history of grocery stores. Over the years, the groceries were also sometimes home to the Post Office sub-station No. 10. Among the early grocers were:

Sherman G. Willard, grocer – building shown in the photo above. Willard ran the grocery and post office here from the mid-1890s to about 1911. Willard later opened a grocery in Knightville at 82 Ocean Street.

Daniel P. Cobb, grocer – about 1912-1916. Cobb's son-in-law Henry Griffin ran the store. Cobb later set up a store at 450 Preble Street;

Clinton E. Wendley, grocer – around 1916-1919;

William W. Arey Variety – at 427 Preble Street, 1921-1924;

Fred W. Richardson, grocer - Fred Richardson moved from 446 Preble to 429 Preble in 1924. He eventually expanded into both the 427 and 429 storefronts. By 1929, he was advertising "groceries, meats, hardware, and notions". By the early 1930s, Richardson was still running this store, but he also became the proprietor of the Willard Inn at the end of Willard Street. After the A&P vacated the store on the other side of Willard Square, Richardson moved his store to that location, around 1941.

The **Willard Square Handy Store** was originally established in 1941 and was located at 427 Preble Street, on the right side of the large building. The store sold meats, groceries, fruits, vegetables, beer and other items. On the left side, at 429 Preble, Warren Wass operated his barber shop for three decades. The building also had a small, one-story structure attached to its left side. Marion Cobb operated **Marion's Beauty Shop** from that small building in the 1940s and 1950s. There were other beauty shops there over the years, among them **Willard Square Beauty Shop** and **Hair on the Square**. The building was later torn down and a driveway now covers the area.

Edward McGonagle was the first proprietor of the Willard Square Handy Store, opening the store's doors in 1941. McGonagle ran the store for just a few years before taking over the Broadway Market at 323 Broadway in 1944. Mrs. Florence Carver was then listed as proprietor for a short time; Pearl Salisbury took over in the mid-1940s. Salisbury ran the store for several years under the name Willard Square Handy Store, before changing the name to **Salisbury's Market** in the late 1940s.

Salisbury's Market was a small store, selling soda, beer and other variety store items. Resident Barbara Hawkes remembers that the store also sold firecrackers on the 4th of July. Pearl Salisbury ran the store until the early 1950s. The building now houses the offices of a building contractor.

A little further down Preble Street is a large apartment building at <u>446 Preble</u>. In early years, a small grocery was operated out of the front of the first floor. Around 1920, **Raymond L. Elliott** operated a store selling groceries, meats and provisions. **Fred W. Richardson** operated his first South Portland grocery from this building around 1922-1923. Richardson had previously run a store on Cumberland Avenue in Portland. About 1924, Richardson moved his store down to 427-429 Preble, and **Carl W. Graves** opened his grocery at 446. For a few years, **George Simonton** (formerly running his barbershop/poolroom at 419 Preble) ran a barbershop from the site (before moving next door), then Griffin's Fish Market was in operation in the 1930s.

Henry Griffin had previously worked in his father-in-law's store at 427 Preble Street, then he operated a store on Willard Beach at the end of Willard Street. He went on to run a grocery at 271 Preble Street with his father, William; they sold that business and opened **Griffin's Fish Market** here around 1934. William Griffin helped out in the store as a fish cutter, until his death in November 1934. Although called Griffin's Fish Market, the store sold a full line of groceries, bread, canned goods and meats. The Griffins lived in an apartment upstairs. Willard Square resident Herbert Pray remembers that his wife Leola (Henry's daughter) used to deliver groceries for the store. According to Pray, Griffin "did a whale of a business on Friday…there were a lot of people in this locality that wouldn't eat anything but fish." Griffin's closed around 1938 and the store space was used as an apartment throughout World War II.

Rice's Cash Market was established at 446 Preble Street around 1946 by Richard "Dick" Rice and his father, Herbert.

Rice's Cash Market after a snow storm.   *Courtesy of David Rice*

Herbert Rice had previously worked in the 1920s and 1930s as a manager for A&P. Dick Rice had served in the Navy as a storekeeper, and upon his return, he worked for a short time as a clerk at F.K. Richards. Rice's Cash

Market was a real family operation, with Herbert's wife and other children also working in the store. Herbert's son, David, was only eight years old when they opened, and was soon stocking shelves and sweeping floors. Herbert Rice, Jr. worked as a printer in Portland, but still pitched in each week to give Dick a night off.

Herbert Rice died in 1949 and Dick continued running the store with his mother and brother, David, active in the operation.

The market carried a full line of items, including canned goods and other grocery-type items, beer, cigarettes and candy, plus there was a large meat counter with fresh meats. Rice's Cash Market also sold firecrackers, which in that era was legal. The store was open from 6:30am to 10pm, seven days a week.

David Rice describes his brother Dick as innovative, creative and hardworking. Dick started off in the store making Italian sandwiches, selling a half-Italian for 20 cents and a whole Italian for 30 cents. Over the years, he developed a large sandwich business. Under the "Kitchen Maid" label, they made and packaged a large variety of sandwiches in the store for customers like the American Legion and to small stores that didn't make their own sandwiches. The store closed around 1956 and was converted into another apartment.

David Rice on the front steps of Rice's Cash Market.   *Courtesy of David Rice*

Next door at 450 Preble Street, Daniel Cobb established a small grocery in 1916. The store ran for about a year, then **Gribbin & Goodnow**, grocers, were in operation until about 1919. The building has remained largely residential since that time.

In the early days, the area from the large building at 450 Preble all the way to Willard Street was a large field, on which Daniel Cobb grew tobacco and had his celery beds right on the corner of Preble and Willard.

12 MONUMENT SQUARE,
PORTLAND, MAINE

The Cobb family was very prominent in the Willard area at the turn of the century. Dan Cobb (left) was a large property owner. According to his granddaughter, Helen, Cobb built the three flat apartment building at 450 Preble, on the site where his parents had previously owned a small cape cod-style house.

Courtesy of Helen Griffin Hurd

He also owned much of the land behind the house, extending all the way down to Willard Beach, where there was a barn, a squash house, a cabbage house, an apple orchard and a bubbling spring surrounded by watercress. It was a large operation with Cobb shipping a lot of his produce down to Boston. According to his granddaughter, Cobb was the first person to grow iceberg lettuce in the East, as it previously was considered a California product.

Daniel Flynn had previously owned a store in Massachusetts before moving to Maine. He went to work for the shipyard during World War II and saved his money. Towards the end of the war, he bought a small cape-style house that was being built on the corner of Preble and Willard Street. After living there for a few years, he built a small store next to the house and opened **Flynn's Variety Store** at 466 Preble. He and his wife Marion ran that store until about 1966, when he sold the house and business to Alan Sawyer.

Courtesy of Elizabeth Flynn Hayman, Barbara Flynn Hawkes, and Daniel Flynn, Jr.

In the early days when they had first opened the store, among other items, Marion Flynn would can peaches and tomatoes and sell them in the store. Other items sold included bread, milk, butter, canned goods, ice cream, and soda. At one point, the Flynns made Italian sandwiches as well.

Daniel Flynn with daughter, Barbara in the doorway of Flynn's Variety, 466 Preble Street

Courtesy of Elizabeth Flynn Hayman, Barbara Flynn Hawkes, and Daniel Flynn, Jr.

After purchasing the home and store, Alan Sawyer and his wife, Evelyn, changed the name to *Sawyer's Variety* and went on to run the little store next to their home until the late 1970s. The space has since been converted and is now part of the living space of the attached home.

Willard Street

The trolley line ran down Willard Street to the beach in the summer and, especially during the Depression years, some residents would run a food stand to make a little extra money. Mrs. Littlejohn ran a small grocery at 45 Willard Street from the late 1920s to the mid-1930s. Resident Mildred Demass also remembers the Jordans on Willard Street. The Jordans' house was set back on the property and there was a small stand up close to the street; the Jordan's son, Ray, sold hot dogs there in the summer in the mid-1930s. Another family also ran a fried clam stand in the summer.

At 49 Willard Street, **Charles F. Rand,** grocer, was run by Charles and his sister Hattie in the 1920s. Their house was next door at 51 Willard Street; the shop was in a separate building with the store in the front room and a small storeroom in the back.

Resident Mildred DeMass remembers that Joseph and Frances Doyle moved in with the Rands in the late 1920s and helped out with the store. After Mr. Rand died in 1930, the Doyles continued operating the shop as *Mrs. Frances Doyle,* grocer, through the 1930s.

The store was primarily a homemade ice cream shop. The Doyles also sold milk, bread, penny candy, cookies and some canned goods. Lois Doyle says that her husband, Archie and his sister, both worked at the shop with their parents. She says that Archie told the story of how one day he was churning ice cream and wanted to go down to Willard Beach with his friends; he rushed the churning and crystals formed in the ice cream. After having to start over and churn a new batch of ice cream, he learned not to rush the process.

After the Doyle's shop closed in the late 1930s, the building was converted to a home that is still there today.

Continuing down Willard Street, on the left side, right on the beach, was a refreshment and ice cream stand, built by *Daniel P. Cobb* around 1906. It was a large two story building with the refreshment stand on the first floor and an apartment upstairs. As he was busy with other ventures, Cobb hired help to staff the facility in the summer.

Griffin's Store on Willard Beach in 1924   *Courtesy of Herb Pray*

Dan Cobb's son-in-law, Henry Griffin ran the operation in the early 1920s. Resident Mildred Demass remembers **Griffin's Store** selling French fries and fried fish. An advertisement from the early 1920s lists "Griffin's Store, Willard Beach - Hot Dogs, Ice Cream, Confectionery, Cold Drinks". After the large two-story structure burned, Henry Griffin built a new building on the Fort Preble side of the original lot, but very close to where the first building was.

Also at the foot of Willard Street, in the 1930s and early 1940s, Sam Silverman ran an operation, then known as the **Willard Beach Bath House** and **Sam's Lunch**. In the mid-1940s, Sarah Profenno was listed as proprietor.

At left in the picture is Dan Cobb's large two-story building and Sam Silverman's is the small building just to its left. The popcorn stand can also be seen at the left edge of the picture.

Courtesy of the South Portland Historical Society

The New Willard Inn and Sam's Pop Corn Stand, at the foot of Willard Street on Willard Beach, in the 1930s.

From the author's collection, an L.N. Mitchell photo

Another building at the foot of Willard Street, on the right side, was the Willard Inn. There were a number of different proprietors over the years. In the 1930s, the inn was run by Fred W. Richardson, who also was the proprietor of Richardson's Market in Willard Square.

In the small building on the beach next to the Willard Inn, Sam Silverman ran a refreshment stand from the mid-1930s to the mid-1940s.

In the early 1970s, the stand was home to *The Dory*, run by Thomas and Alice Carmody. The Carmodys sold foods like hot dogs, clam cakes, French fries, onion rings, popcorn, and drinks to beachgoers in the summer. After the Carmodys closed The Dory, the stand never again housed a food operation. The stand still sits on the beach, although the sand now reaches halfway up the small building.

Sam Silverman's Pop Corn Stand on Willard Beach in 1938, where Earle Angell had his first job.   *Courtesy of Sylvia Angell*

Samuel Silverman

Sam Silverman is described as quite a character. Residents who remember him have a wide range of stories about Silverman's antics to draw a crowd to his summer operations. One common story surrounds the competitions that Silverman would put on for the kids. There were swimming races and many remember the "greasy pole" that was set up for beachgoers to try to climb and reach a prize at the top. Silverman also kept animals in cages, including a bear, and a monkey named Bridget that would "raise the devil". Residents remember a seal, as well, but there are contradictory reports as to whether the seal showed up on its own, or whether Silverman kept it there. It was a fun place, nonetheless.

In later years, Sam Silverman ran various beano operations around South Portland, including at the Willard Inn, the Willard Hose House and the Car Barn in Knightville.

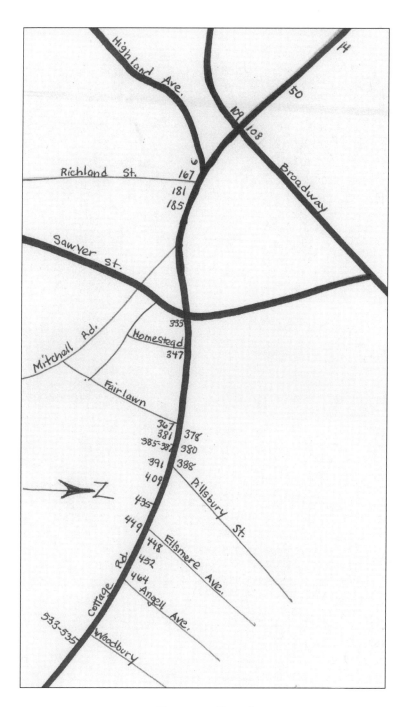

Cottage Road

Four

Cottage Road

From the border of South Portland and Cape Elizabeth to Legion Square in Knightville, Cottage Road has been a busy thoroughfare throughout the past century.

Cape Shore Pharmacy and First National Stores in the 1940s
Courtesy of the City of South Portland

Right on the Cape Elizabeth border, at <u>533-535 Cottage Road</u>, the *Cape Shore Pharmacy* was run by Raymond Pooler from the 1930s through early 1950s. The pharmacy then became *Andrews Cape Shore Pharmacy* and continued operating into the 1970s, then became *Jones Cape Shore Pharmacy* in the 1970s, '80s and into the 1990s. *The Stitching Mantis* now occupies the site.

The building also has housed a long history of grocery stores:
Ottawa Park Market – around 1908-1909;
Harry W. Dunton, grocer – around 1915-1916;
Fred K. Swett Co., grocer – about 1917;
Ernest E. Blake, grocer - about 1919;
Scribner Company – around 1920-1921. The store was run by Dow C. Scribner. In South Portland's 25th Anniversary Program in 1920, Scribner Company is listed as selling "groceries, fruits, home cooked foods, ice cream & sodas, drug store sundries."
Clarence A. Wardwell, grocer – about 1922;
Robert G. Elliot, grocer – around 1923-1926 at 535 Cottage;

First National Stores – late 1930s to late 1940s, moved here from 464 Cottage Road;

Gehrke's Nation Wide Store – around 1949-1950; and

Town Line Shop – early 1950s, clothing store run by Floyd and Beatrice Richards. They then moved their shop to 449 Cottage Road.

Edward Cook with his son, Edward, Jr., standing in front of their residence at 452 Cottage Road. The building down the sidewalk in this picture is an apartment building at 464 Cottage, on the corner of Angell Avenue, with a variety store on the first floor.   Courtesy of Doris Cook

At 464 Cottage Road, on the corner of Cottage Road and Angell Avenue, there used to be a three-story apartment building with a small grocery on site. The old building was much closer to the road than the current Drillen building.

A sampling of storekeepers at the site would include the following:

Blake's Home Bakery and Provisions, Frazier & Mitchell, C. Nielsen, and *Emil Wernig* – in the 1920s. These four consecutive shopkeepers were bakers and sold a full line of bakery products and some groceries;

First National Stores - early to mid-1930s. Around 1937, First National moved down the street to 535 Cottage Road;

Darling's Market – about 1937. Winfield Darling previously ran a store in Willard Square, then ran a store at 49 Angell Avenue before moving to this site;

Stinson's Grocery - about 1938, run by Howard Stinson;

Community Store – late 1930s to mid-1940s, run by Herbert Pitts;

Rene's Cash Market - around 1945-1946, run by Rene Levesque;
Brown's Market - around 1947-1948, run by Harold Brown;
Jay's Market - about 1949, run by J. Edward Lang;
Jim's Market - about 1950, run by Vincent Papi;
William T. Whitlock - about 1951, a grocer;

Richard and Loretta Schools inside their Cottage Road Variety at 464 Cottage Road in 1969. The store sold pizza, Italian sandwiches, meatball and sausage sandwiches, beer and soda, bread, candy, cigarettes, and other grocery products. *Courtesy of Portland Press Herald*

Then in the early 1950s, the store at 460-464 Cottage Road became known as ***Cottage Road Variety***. The operators of Cottage Road Variety included R. William Papi (around 1952-1955), Assunta Ferrante (around 1956-1958), Anthony Nappi (around 1959-1967), Coley Welch* (about 1968), and Richard Schools (around 1969-1970).

> *Coley Welch was one of the world's top ranked middleweight boxers in the 1940s; he became the New England Middleweight Champion in 1941. According to Richard Schools, businessman Harold Foley had leased the store and hired Coley Welch to run it around 1968. Welch ran the store for a short time, then Foley hired Schools to take over the business.

According to Anthony Nappi, his grandmother, Sue Ferrante ran the Cottage Road Variety, then would later go on to run Sue's Variety from 385 Cottage Road. Nappi says that while his father, Anthony, was running the store, his grandmother lived upstairs and when it got busy, they would just bang on the pipes and she would come down to lend a hand. The store sold Italian sandwiches and carried an extensive selection of beer and wine. Many customers would stop in on their way to Fort Williams.

The store was closed and the building demolished in early 1970. A shed on the site was also demolished in 1972 and the lot was left vacant for many years. **Drillen Hardware** had already been operating further down and across the street at 433 Cottage Road; the Drillens built a new building on this corner and opened here in 1986.

Like its neighbor at 464 Cottage Road, the building at 452 Cottage was a large building with many apartments, with its front steps right up close to the street. Around 1904, brothers Charles and Wilfred Tarling opened **Tarling Bros. Groceries** at 452 Cottage Road. By about 1906, Wilfred had left the business and moved to Boston. Charles Tarling would continue operating the grocery, with his brothers Walter and Arthur, until the mid-1910s.

After Tarling Bros. closed, the building was used primarily as apartments up into the 1960s. The building was later demolished and a new building, which would house the Laundercenter, was built further back on the lot. The current building now houses Neighborhood Laundry.

Tarling Bros. Groceries at 452 Cottage Road.   *Courtesy of Judith Kelley*

At 448 Cottage Road, the **Elsmere Garage** opened in 1921, managed by John Baker. Baker would go on in the mid-1920s to take over the operation and name it **John R. Baker Autos**. Before World War II, several other automobile repair and sales businesses occupied the space, including Beesley's Garage, Young's Garage, Kennedy's Garage, and Gilbert & Harris Garage.

Elsmere Garage in 1921.   *Courtesy of the South Portland Historical Society*

Colonial Cleaners at 448 Cottage Road.   *Courtesy of Doris Cook*

After the building at 448 Cottage was left vacant during World War II, a new business opened: ***Nelson W. Dyer Cleaners***. Dyer Cleaners operated for several years before the long-running ***Colonial Cleaners*** opened in November 1949. It turned out to be a good use of the space, as Colonial Cleaners operated there for the rest of the century. ***Pratt-Abbott*** now occupies the building.

The Town Line Shop moved to <u>449 Cottage Road</u> in the mid-1950s from its previous location at 535 Cottage Road. Run by Floyd and Beatrice Richards, this clothing store operated from this location for about three years, then Dr. John Boland moved his dental practice here from across the street at 458 Cottage. Dr. Boland served the community from this building well into the 1980s. The site was originally home to a Sunoco service station. According to Dr. Boland's daughter, Barbara, her father later had the underground tanks removed. The building is now home to the dental practice of Dr. Ortengren.

Courtesy of the Dr. John Boland family

Pork loins were only 29 cents a pound in this 1955 photo of the Cape Red & White Super Market at <u>435 Cottage Road</u>. The store was in business for over two decades, from the late 1940s to about 1970. There have been a wide range of businesses since then, including Columbia Market, L'il Peach Convenience Store, Tommy's Pizza & Sausage, and a day care center. The current occupants are Thai Taste and Show Time Video.

Courtesy of the City of South Portland

One can hardly imagine how many loads of laundry have been washed at the Cape Launderette, 409 Cottage Road, since this early circa 1949 picture was taken. Courtesy of the City of South Portland

Early photo of Cape Veterinary Clinic, 391 Cottage Road. Cape Vet opened in the late 1950s; the site had previously been home to a number of Texaco and other service stations in the 1940s and 1950s.
Courtesy of the City of South Portland

Circa 1990 photo of DiPietro's Market and Show Time Video on Meeting House Hill. Courtesy of the City of South Portland

Now site of *DiPietro's Market*, the building at 385-387 Cottage Road has had many occupants over the years. The original store opened in the late 1930s, *Mileson's Market* run by William L. Mileson. Mileson had previously operated a store a few buildings down at 377 Cottage Road in the early 1930s (*William L. Mileson Restaurant* around 1933, and then *William L. Mileson Grocer*).

This 1940s photo shows 385-387 Cottage Road. Martin's 5¢ & $1.00 Store was located on the left side of the building and Mileson's Market was on the right side.

Courtesy of the City of South Portland

For many years, the 385-387 Cottage Road building was split into two stores:

On the right side of the building:
In the late 1940s, Mileson's Market was replaced by *Shaw's Market*, run by Norman Shaw; Shaw's operated there until the mid-1950s. James Lynds ran *Lynd's Market* from the mid-1950s to the mid-1960s, Sue Ferrante ran *Sue's Variety* in the late '60s to early '70s, and Jim Langella ran *Langella's* for a short time. When Sam DiPietro's Market took over the space, the dividing wall was knocked down.

On the left side of the building:
Martin's 5¢ & $1.00 Store (Norman M. Martin, proprietor) operated from the site during the 1940s, then moved across the street around 1950 to 378 Cottage Road, which had just been vacated by the A&P. After Martin's moved, there were several businesses at 387 Cottage over the next two decades: *E.L. Watkins* cleaners, the Old North Gift Shop, and Coin-op Kleanerrette.

*This building at **381 Cottage Road** sat just to the right of what is now the DiPietro's building. The Cape Cod Bakery operated here from the late 1940s to the late 1950s. The Nu Again Shoppe had previously operated from the building at the corner of Cottage and Angell Ave.; the clothing store moved here around 1960 and ran for about five years. After the building burned, the land became part of DiPietro's parking lot.*

Courtesy of the City of South Portland

Where **Barbara's Kitchen & Café** now stands at 388 Cottage Road, there have been a variety of businesses. The **A&P** operated from this location before moving to 378 Cottage Road in the late 1920s. **George F. Hilborn's Bakery** was here in the 1930s; later the site housed Contoure Beauty Salon and then Chester "Chuck" Konecki tailor shop.

The storefront at 380 Cottage Road was home to druggists for many decades. **Donald F. Melcher** operated his drugstore there in the mid-1920s, and **Joseph J. Lemellin** had his drugstore there in the late 1920s, up until the long-running Cottage Road Pharmacy opened in the early 1930s.

The **Cottage Road Pharmacy** at 380 Cottage Road was first operated by John Cassidy from the early 1930s until the mid-1950s. Most residents referred to it as "Cassidy's" even though the signage said Cottage Road Pharmacy. Around 1957, Frederick and Gordon Prescott took over the pharmacy. They changed the name to **Prescott's Pharmacy** around 1960 and continued operating from this location until around 1966 when they built a new pharmacy across the street at 367 Cottage Road, on the corner of Fairlawn Avenue.

After Prescott's Pharmacy moved out, the "pharmacy era" of that storefront ended; businesses operating from that site since then have included Ray's Radio & TV Service, Show Time Video, and Trademark, Inc.

The *Great Atlantic & Pacific Tea Company (A&P)* store on Meeting House Hill was originally located at 125 Pillsbury Street, roughly in the area where Barbara's Kitchen now stands at 388 Cottage Road. The A&P operated from that site for a very short time, then moved to the storefront at 378 Cottage Road where it ran from the late 1920s and on through the 1940s. This A&P was typical of one of the early groceries: clerks would wait on customers and there was no self-service.

The A&P store and the Cottage Road Pharmacy on Meeting House Hill.
Courtesy of Sylvia Angell

After the A&P closed, Norman Martin moved his *Martin's 5¢ and $1.00 Store* here from its former location across the street. Martin's operated here through the 1950s and there have been a number of other businesses since then, including *Dolly's Hobby Shop* and *Carolyn's Caterers.*

According to resident Parker Wells, the old three-flat apartment building that had been located on the corner of Cottage and Fairlawn, at 367 Cottage Road, was torn down in the 1960s to make way for a new drugstore. *Prescott's Pharmacy* had operated across the street at 380 Cottage Road. The Prescotts had a new brick building erected and opened here in the mid-1960s. The pharmacy continued in operation until the mid-1970s.

Prescott's Pharmacy carried a large line of pharmacy items, including prescriptions, cosmetics, gifts and cards. The store also featured a luncheonette.

In the early 1940s, *William L. Mileson* ran a small ice cream store at 347 Cottage Road; Mileson's nephew, Richard remembers that there was a field here with the ice cream shop located in a small wooden building in the middle of the field. In the mid-1940s, Mileson built a new building and started the much-loved *Hill Top Tea Room*, which served lunches, Italian sandwiches and ice cream.

Storefront at 347 Cottage Road   *Courtesy of the City of South Portland*

In the 1950s, Lloyd W. Johnson ran the *Hill Top Coffee Shop* from the site. The shop served coffee, doughnuts and other pastries, as well as homemade ice cream. In May 1959, the Hill Top Coffee Shop applied for a permit to install a new roof that would extend to the sidewalk, so that it could offer curb service to its customers. A number of other businesses have operated here over the years, including *Hill's Shoe Shop*, *The Foyer*, *Dyer's Flower Shop*, and at present, *The Buttered Biscuit*.

Around 1919, *George E. Haggett* opened his grocery at 333 Cottage Road. In 1920, he advertised "groceries & provisions, fruit, confectionery, ice cream and cigars". Haggett closed his store around 1924. He would later operate a store at 185 Preble Street, as well as the Broadway Market at 323 Broadway.

Walter B. Carpenter then ran a grocery from the site in the mid-1920s and *Dennison's Cash Market* opened around 1929. As described in a 1929 South Portland High School yearbook, Dennison's offered the "best quality meats, native poultry, fancy groceries, and vegetables". Around 1932, *Ernest A. Bean* ran a grocery, then *Coles P. Flewelling Grocery* the year after that. In the mid-1930s to the early 1940s, *Cottage Road Market* was in operation. It was the last grocery at this address.

Dyer's Flower Shop operated from this site for many years before moving down to 347 Cottage Road. The Beecher Agency/Coldwell Banker

Beecher Real Estate was located here for many years and Coast Line Credit Union now occupies the 333 portion of the building.

333 Cottage Road *was originally the site of numerous groceries over the years. In this aerial photo of Meeting House Hill, the First Congregational Church can be seen at the top of the picture, Mount Pleasant Cemetery is on the right, and the white house in the lower right is 333 Cottage Road. The house has since been replaced by a long brick building.*

Courtesy of the South Portland Historical Society

At 185 Cottage Road, *Joseph H. Harrigan* ran a grocery business in the early 1920s. Around 1924, Malcolm F. Bishop, a partner in Brown & Bishop (a company which also ran two stores on Congress Street in Portland), opened a store here and ran it until about 1927 under what appears to be the *Brown & Bishop* name. The store name then changed to *Hillside Market* with Malcolm Bishop listed as its proprietor. In 1927 and 1929, Bishop was advertising his Hillside Market at this address, selling groceries, meats, fish and provisions.

Around 1932, Bishop moved his store next door to 181 Cottage Road and *Cape City Market* opened at 185 Cottage. Around 1934, *Ames & Faraday Grocers* was in operation here, and then that store moved to 181 Cottage. Around 1935, *Superba Grocery Store* was in operation at 183 Cottage Road, believed to be another number for this building. That store was run by Spencer Brookes and carried groceries and bakery products.

Another *Hillside Market* was established in the late 1930s by George Standley. Sooren Mardigan bought it in the mid-1940s and operated it as the *Hillside Red & White Market*. His son, Ed Mardigan, took over the business after Sooren's death in 1962.

Hillside Red & White Market at the bottom of Meeting House Hill
Courtesy of the City of South Portland

Like many neighborhood grocers, Hillside Red & White succumbed to the larger supermarkets and closed its doors in the mid-1970s. Several other businesses have since operated from this site, including The Tux Shop, *House of Weddings, Gingiss Formal Wear* and The Hair Force. In 1986, *Cherished Possessions* opened here.

185 Cottage Road   *Portland Press Herald/Charles H. Merrill photo, 1982*

The original Hillside Market at <u>181 Cottage Road</u>, to the right of where the Hillside Red & White would later open. Hillside Market started operation next door at 185 Cottage in the early 1920s, then moved here around 1932.

Courtesy of the City of South Portland

The Hillside Market at 181 Cottage Road closed around 1934 and **Ames & Faraday Grocers** moved from next door into this space. Laurel T. Ames, the proprietor, lived in the upstairs apartment and operated the store until around 1943. After he closed the store, the downstairs remained vacant for a few years. Around 1947, William and Maria Menneally opened **Menneally's Nation Wide Store**. They lived upstairs until the store closed a few years later.

Alvah and Norman Robinson, brothers, came down from Bangor and took over the store around 1950, opening **Robinson Bros. Nation Wide Store**. They lived upstairs with their families until about 1957 when they moved to a house on the corner of Highland and Ocean Street.

Around 1961, the Robinsons took a break from the store and **Millie's Nation Wide Store** operated for just a few years, before Robinson Bros. opened up again around 1964. The Robinsons ran the store until the early 1970s when they sold the property. Holy Cross Credit Union later occupied the space and the building has since been torn down.

When Leonard "Red" Bolling built this Tastee Freez franchise at <u>167 Cottage Road</u> in 1952, he began a South Portland tradition. For years, people of all ages enjoyed frozen treats from the Tastee Freez, and when Bolling dropped the franchise and renamed the store Red's Dairy Freeze, the customers kept coming. Red's son, Chris Bolling, has continued running this landmark ice cream shop since the 1980s.

Courtesy of the City of South Portland

At <u>6 Highland Avenue</u>, just to the right of Tastee Freez in the early 1950s was **William L. Mileson's Variety Store**. Mileson's nephew, Richard Mileson, remembers that his uncle sold just about everything in that store, including fireworks. This was the last of William Mileson's many stores in South Portland; he died in 1955.

After Mileson's variety store closed, the building was demolished and a small building was moved to the site from atop Meeting House Hill. **Alfred and Mildred Niles** operated a small restaurant from the site in the mid-1950s. In the late 1950s, **Tomaso Degifico** is listed as a barber at 6 Highland Avenue, and there have been barbers and/or beauticians operating from the site ever since.

Although the corner of Broadway and Cottage has been home to Pratt Abbott Cleaners since the 1960s, 109 Cottage Road was originally home to the long-running Trefethen's Garage. The advertisement below appeared in the 1947 cookbook "Someone's in the Kitchen".

Courtesy of the First Congregational Church

At 108 Cottage Road, on another corner of Broadway and Cottage Road, where the Mill Cove Apartment building now rises, there was originally a much smaller apartment building on the site. In the early 1950s, the **Corner Variety Store** was in business in that building.

Martin's Food Mart was the first grocery to open at 50 Cottage Road in the mid-1960s. Martin's was part of a grocery chain owned by John Martin. The store has undergone much change since its early beginnings. **Wellby Super Drug** operated from the site for a time, as well as a savings and loan. The store later became **Martin's Shop 'N Save** and now is known as **Hannaford Supermarket.**

Going back in time, this site was originally part of the shore line until much of the land was filled. The **Old Sparhawk Mills** rug manufacturer had been located at 60 Cottage Road in the 1930s through early 1960s; that would be roughly in the parking lot, in front and a little to the right of today's Hannaford Supermarket.

At 14 Cottage Road, **Cape City Service Station** was in operation in the 1930s. **Higgins Motor Sales** was in business here in the 1940s. During the 1950s, three consecutive businesses ran from the building: **Knightville Garage, Mill Creek Motors**, and then the **Knightville Car Wash. South Portland Supply Company** was the first of several plumbing companies to conduct business from the site in the 1960s. Other businesses at the site over the years include Sentinel Fire Safety, Mill Creek TV Repair, and Drake Equipment Company.

This 1960s photo shows the Philip E. Baker Co. at 14 Cottage Road. Maynard W. Waltz Heating & Plumbing later occupied the space. The original building was set back from the road quite a bit. Around 1976, an addition was built on to the front of the building. South Portland Sewing Center moved in to the expanded building in 1976 and is still operating from the left side of the facility. The right side of the building has had a number of tenants over the years, including My Sister's Closet.

Courtesy of the City of South Portland

On one corner of Legion Square, the first building on Cottage Road is the Casco Bank building at 2 Cottage Road. At that site in the 1910s, there was a grocer, **George E. Calderwood**, operating from that site, albeit briefly. The adjoining buildings to the right of Casco Bank are 4, 6, and 8 Cottage Road. That string of buildings has housed a multitude of businesses over the years, including Builders Hardware Supply, Rod's TV, Phinney Florist, and Legion Square Florist, to name a few.

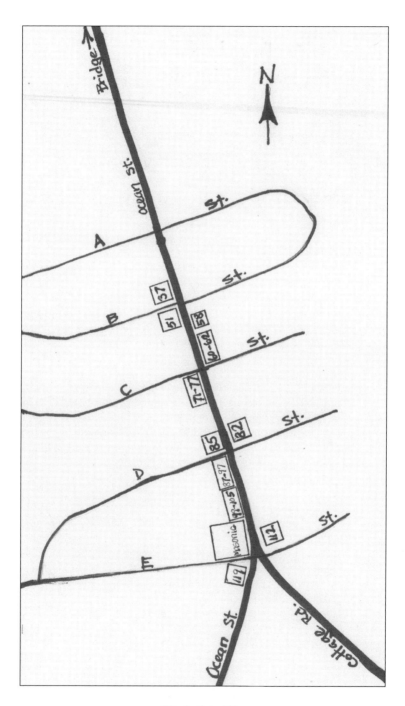

Knightville

Five

Knightville

Master shipwright Thomas Knight established a shipyard in 1850 on the Cape Elizabeth side of the Portland Bridge. By 1875, the busy little village was named Knightville, in honor of Thomas Knight.

Knightville has undergone an incredible amount of change over the years. At the turn of the century, the trolley ran through the village on its way to and from Portland via the Portland Bridge. Whether by horse, buggy, trolley or foot, people who needed to get from South Portland and Cape Elizabeth to Portland and beyond would all head through Knightville to get to their destination. The streets of Knightville were lined with elm trees and stately homes. There were many groceries set up along Ocean Street to serve the people passing through.

After the construction of the Million Dollar Bridge in 1916, and as the use of automobiles became more common, the neighborhood underwent a major transformation. As the decades passed, many of the large homes on Ocean Street began to disappear, replaced by service stations, restaurants and other businesses. Through World War II, Knightville endured significant change, and some would argue that the area lost its "neighborhood feel".

In 1997, the Casco Bay Bridge opened, thrusting Knightville into a new era of change. The traffic that had passed through the heart of the neighborhood was now gone; the new bridge bypassed the area and traffic is now sent directly to Broadway. Although some stores did close, the neighborhood has responded with a new sense of energy and direction. New businesses have come, much investment has restored the buildings and infrastructure, and the neighborhood has reinvented itself as the "new" downtown of South Portland.

Looking towards the water on E Street circa 1905.   *Author's collection*

January 1924 photo of the Stewart P. Morrill Post at 20 E Street. The name Legion Square was derived from the American Legion that resided in this building for many years. Later on, the building housed a restaurant, Lewis Furniture Mart, and some other businesses. Wall-Marr Ceramic Studio now occupies the facility.

Courtesy of the Portland Press Herald

This advertisement for the Lewis Furniture Mart appeared in the 1947 Someone's in the Kitchen cookbook.

Courtesy of the First Congregational Church

Children walking across Legion Square from the old Knightville School. The Knightville School was located right across the square, on the corner where the Post Office parking lot now stands. Thomas Devine's Pharmacy is the long building running from the center to the right side of this photo detail. Note the original homes running down Ocean Street from the pharmacy.

Collections of Maine Historical Society

Across Legion Square at 112 Ocean Street sat a large building that was home to drugstores in earlier years. In the 1890s, the **S.S. Lightbody & Co.** drugstore was in operation on this corner. By 1901, **Gregory E. Blish,** druggist, was operating the store. In the early 1900s, Gregory Blish also served on South Portland's Board of Health.

Around 1908, **Thomas F. Devine** took over the drugstore and ran it for over two decades. Residents have referred to Thomas Devine's as an upscale pharmacy, with a very "formal" feel inside. In addition to prescriptions and a soda fountain, the store sold fine quality stationery, school books and other school supplies.

After Devine closed the store in the mid-1930s, Henry Alix ran his **Henry's Café** from the site for a few years. The building was later torn down to make way for a service station. There have been several service stations at the site. In more recent years, **Elaine's Beauty Salon** operated from this location. It is now home to **Bayside Hair Salon.**

In this June 1978 photograph of Legion Square, Nanos Variety can be seen on the left, with the Masonic building just to the right of Nanos.
Courtesy of the Portland Press Herald

On another corner of Legion Square, starting back in the late 1800s, **George Stevens** lived at <u>119 Ocean Street</u> and ran a grocery store from the first floor. He closed the store around 1908 and the building was used as a residence for many years. About 1934, Stephen Nanos bought the building and established **Stephen Nanos Variety Store**. Stephen and his wife, Sophia, ran the store through the 1930s.

Upon Stephen's retirement, his brother, Harry Nanos took over the store. **Harry Nanos Grocery** was in operation during WWII. Toward the end of the war, Phil Notis and a partner, Steve Christie, bought the business and ran **Nanos Grocery Store** until around 1950. Phil Notis then sold his share in the business to Steve Notis (no relation) and Phil started his own variety store down at 75 Ocean Street.

Since Nanos Variety had started back in 1934, the little store had sold the usual small variety items. While Steve Notis was running the operation, he introduced Italian sandwiches, and later pizza. According to Steve Notis' wife, Irene, the store was open seven days a week.

In 1962, Loucas Prodromou bought the store from Steve Notis. Prodromou proceeded to run it under the name **Nanos Variety** for over three decades himself. Since he sold the business in 1993, there have been a few different owners. **Barb's Breakfast and Lunch** is now located in the building.

This early photo of the Masonic Building, at 107-111 Ocean Street, shows the South Portland Branch Post Office on the first floor. In the 1940s, Cushman Baking operated from this building. Notice the home on the right that no longer exists.

Courtesy of the Portland Press Herald

Starting in Legion Square on the corner of E Street, there is at present a long series of interconnected buildings which reaches from the Masonic Building all the way down to D Street. The storefronts are numbered from 87 to 105 Ocean Street. In the earlier days, there were several different free standing buildings here.

First National Stores first appeared in Knightville around 1927 at 95 Ocean Street; it moved up to 105 Ocean Street (right next to the Masonic Building) around 1933 and remained there until the mid-1950s. It then moved to 161 Ocean Street. ***Whitten's Appliances*** operated from the site for a year around 1955. ***Sherwin-Williams*** would later occupy the space.

Shortly after First National Stores moved in to 105 Ocean Street, ***Henry's Log Cabin Lunch*** opened at 103 Ocean Street around 1935. The business was located inside a small log cabin building on the site. In the 1935 SPHS yearbook, Henry's Log Cabin advertised "Italian sandwiches, hot hamburgers, and pepper steaks". The restaurant was run by Henry Brosseau. In the early 1940s, Brosseau closed this restaurant and started a new Henry's Log Cabin business in Scarborough. The actual log cabin building was moved down to 60 Ocean Street, nestled in next to Dyer & McLaughlin's grocery.

After the log cabin was moved, First National Stores expanded into the space. ***Stuart's Mens Shop*** would later occupy the site.

This photograph from January 1983 shows South Portland Health Services in residence in the Masonic Building, at 109 Ocean Street. The next building down, 103-105 Ocean Street, has been divided into two stores: Sherwin Williams and Stuart's Mens Shop. Smaha's Legion Square Market is in the storefront just beyond Stuart's, and had expanded from 101 Ocean Street into the storefront at 99 Ocean Street as well.

Courtesy of the Portland Press Herald

Around 1936, about a year after Henry's Log Cabin had opened, the Great Atlantic & Pacific Tea Company would open an **A&P** store at 101 Ocean Street, the next storefront down. The A&P operated there for a few years before moving in the late 1930s to its long-running Thomas Street location, across from Uncle Andy's. The A&P site was then taken over by **Columbia Market**.

According to Tom Smaha, his uncle Herbert Smaha moved up from Lawrence, MA in the 1930s and started the first Columbia Market on the first floor of the Columbia Hotel on Congress Street. The South Portland store opened around 1938 at 101 Ocean Street. Herbert's brother, John Smaha bought the store the following year and changed the name to **Smaha's Legion Square Market**.

The current owner, Tom Smaha took over the store operation when his father John retired around 1967. Smaha's Legion Square Market is the longest continuous-running grocery in the city.

On the left side of this circa 1955 photo, Whitten's can be seen taking up two storefronts. To the right of Whitten's is Smaha's Legion Square Market, and to the right of that is F.G. Carr's, the store with the awning.

Courtesy of the Portland Press Herald

Around 1937, the next store down at 99 Ocean Street became the site of **Ben Franklin Stores**. That store would operate for a decade, then was replaced by **F.G. Carr 5¢ to $1.00 Store** around 1947.

This advertisement appeared in the 1947 cookbook Someone's in the Kitchen.

Courtesy of the First Congregational Church

Although connected to the other stores, the Richards Block was built in the 1920s and encompasses the 87-97 Ocean Street storefronts.

At 97 Ocean Street, **Knight Hardware & Paint** opened in the late 1920s and operated for just a couple of years. **Popular Meat Market** occupied the site in the early 1930s, then **Legion Square Pharmacy** opened there around 1934, operated by Albert Wheeler and Nelson Packhem.

Resident Belle Graney remembers working a couple of summers at the pharmacy. "They sold ice cream sundaes and at that time you had syrup for coke," she says. "People would come in and ask for a cherry coke or a lemon coke, and you'd put the syrup in the glass, and then a dash of lemon or cherry or whatever they'd want, and then fill it with soda water…they sold prescriptions and had the soda fountain."

Around the start of World War II, Legion Square Pharmacy moved to 85 Ocean Street. They were replaced by the long-running **Stuart's Mens Shop**. Operated by Louis Gordon, Stuart's Mens Shop remained here selling men's clothing until the late 1950s when it moved to 103 Ocean Street. Later stores at 97 Ocean include **Bike & Blade Sportscenter** and the current **Port Grooming & Pet Care Center**.

As previously mentioned, **First National Stores** opened at 95 Ocean around 1927 and operated from this site until around 1933. As it would happen, 1933 also marked the year that beer sales were legalized and a number of resulting businesses followed at this site: the **Knightville Pool Parlor** in 1933, **Reilly & McNulty Beer** in 1934, and **Michael H. Reilly Beer** in 1935. Around 1936, Harold Richards opened **The Champ** restaurant at 95 Ocean. Although the operators changed over the years, The Champ remained in business there through the mid-1960s. In 1966, Eddie Griffin bought the restaurant and renamed it **The Dugout Sports Grill**. In the 1970s, Griffin bought his buildings at 60-62 Ocean Street and moved The Dugout to that building.

Within a year after **William Tibbets, Jr**. had opened his confectionery at 93 Ocean Street in the late 1920s, he closed and the **Gray Surf Gift Shop** set up its operation. The Gray Surf would operate for three decades from this storefront.

The storefront at 91 Ocean Street has seen a wide variety of businesses over the years. A watchmaker, a cleaning business, **Cushman Baking** around 1933, barber and beauty shops through the 1930s and '40s, and the **Terry Ann Shop** (infant and children's wear) all operated from the site. In later years, H&R Block and then Edward Jones Investments occupied the space

At 89 Ocean Street, **Cape City Meat Market** opened in the late 1920s and operated for just a short time. The site was subsequently home to various shoe repair shops for decades.

Originally home to **Archer's Pool Room** in the late 1920s, the storefront at 87 Ocean Street also served as home to **Inness Photo Service** for many years. Inness started its long association with South Portland when it first opened at 79 Ocean Street in the mid-1930s. After moving to 87 Ocean Street around 1938, it remained here for over a decade, moving to 160 Ocean Street around 1955.

Author photo

At the turn of the 20th century, this building on the corner of D Street was already home to a well-established grocery: **John A.S. Dyer & Co.** The store was in operation as far back as 1890. An advertisement in a 1910 school publication touted, "J.A.S. Dyer & Co., Fancy Groceries, Provisions, Etc., <u>85 Ocean Street</u>, South Portland." Around the late 1930s, the store's name changed to **J.A.S. Dyer's Sons**. Around the start of World War II, J.A.S. Dyer's Sons closed and the Legion Square Pharmacy moved into the space.

May 2005 photo, formerly site of J.A.S. Dyer and Legion Square Pharmacy.

Legion Square Pharmacy had previously been operating up the street at 97 Ocean Street. Albert Wheeler and Nelson Packhem owned and operated the business. Legion Square Pharmacy operated from 85 Ocean Street into the early 1960s, run first by Wheeler and Packhem, and later by pharmacist Leroy Dyment.

At <u>82 Ocean Street</u>, across from Legion Square Pharmacy, in a building that is long since gone, the **Knightville Grocery Company** was in operation during the 1910s, run by William Keith. In a 1910 high school newsletter, the Knightville Grocery touted itself as a dealer in foreign and domestic fancy groceries, also selling fresh oysters, clams and meats.

From about 1914 to 1917, **Sherman G. Willard** took over the operation of the Knightville Grocery; Willard had previously run a store in Willard Square. Around 1918, **Minot Howe** ran his grocery store at 82 Ocean, then **Harrison Bailey** operated a grocery there around 1919.

In 1920, **Robert E. Wilson** started a bakery at 82 Ocean Street. By the late 1920s, the bakery had become **Wilson's Family Bakery** which continued in business through the 1930s. In the early 1940s, **A.E. Ross Bakery** was in operation for a short time, followed by **Neuts Bakery** which was located there from about 1942 to 1946. After Neuts closed, the building was home to a barber/beauty shop and a tailor shop.

The Notis family has long been part of the food scene in South Portland. The photo above shows Tony Notis inside his Bridgeway Restaurant. The long-running business is still in operation at 71-77 Ocean Street, with Tony's son, Alex, now at the helm.

Courtesy of the Notis family

Back in the early 1950s, Tony Notis' father, Philip Notis, established *Phil's Grocery Store* at 75 Ocean Street. His store was located in roughly the spot where the bar is in the restaurant today. Phil Notis ran his grocery until about 1963; he had previously been a partner in Nanos Grocery Store.

On the corner of Ocean and C Street, 62 Ocean Street was originally a grocery store. *John W. Blake,* grocer, was in operation at the turn of the century. Around 1905, *Arthur W. Blake*, grocer, took over and ran the store for the rest of that decade. *Skillin & Knight*, and later *Skillin Bros.,* would operate the grocery through the 1910s.

Knight & McCabe Grocers then opened, and was run by Percy Knight and Lawrence McCabe through the 1920s. In the early 1930s, *Lawrence J. McCabe* operated the store under his own name. He then moved and ran a grocery later in Pleasantdale at 811 Broadway. From about 1933 to 1942, *Dyer & McLaughlin Grocery* was in operation.

Around 1941, Dyer & McLaughlin had the old log cabin moved down the street from its former site at 101/103 Ocean Street. The little building was tucked in next to the larger store and continued operating as *The Log Cabin Restaurant* into the 1970s.

After Dyer & McLaughlin's closed at 62 Ocean Street, Lloyd Alexander moved his *Alexander's Barber Shop* into the building and stayed there through the 1940s, '50s and '60s. He shared the space while he was there, first with *Margaret's Beauty Shop*, then *Alexandria's Beauty Lounge* in the late 1940s, *Elaine's Beauty Lounge* in the early-to-mid-1950s, and Rita's Beauty Lounge in the late 1950s and 1960s.

Margaret's Beauty Shop operated in the early-to-mid-1940s at 62 Ocean Street, sharing the space with Alexander's Barber Shop.

Photos courtesy of David Soule

In 1974, Eddie Griffin purchased the buildings at 60-62 Ocean Street. He leased the restaurant at 60 Ocean for a few years; the site was known as *P & J's Restaurant* during the mid-1970s. Since P & J's Restaurant closed in the late 1970s, there have been a number of different restaurants over the years, including the *Homeplate Restaurant*, *The Log Cabin Restaurant* (again), and *Uncle Billy's Southside BBQ*.

When Griffin purchased the building in 1974, Griffin moved his Griffin's Dugout into the building at 62 Ocean. It remained *Eddie Griffin's Dugout* throughout the 1970s and 1980s, and then changed to *The Griffin Club*. The Griffin Club is still in operation in the same building, and is now run by Marge Griffin.

The Griffin Club in 2005, at 60-62 Ocean Street   *Author photo*

Mooradian Bros. actually began as a grocery a few buildings down at 50 Ocean Street in the late 1920s. Armenag and Gaspar Mooradian moved Mooradian Bros. to 58 Ocean Street in the mid-1930s. In the late 1930s, they changed the name of the store to *Supreme Food*, but continued to operate it themselves. In the early 1940s, they changed the name back to Mooradian Bros.

Mooradian's operated as an IGA store for much of its history. In the 1953 SPHS yearbook, they advertised "Mooradian Brothers – groceries, meats, fruits, ice cream, tonic and tobacco".

Mooradian Bros. store at 58 Ocean Street. Mooradian's operated into the late 1950s.

Courtesy of David Soule,

In the early 1960s, the store at 58 Ocean was remodeled into a restaurant and ***The 707 Restaurant*** was established by Alexander Seader III; Seader had previously operated the Shangri-La Restaurant at 52 Ocean. The 707 Restaurant operated throughout the 1960s and into the mid-1970s, when it was joined by ***Smitty's 707 Tavern***. After the restaurant closed around 1976, the tavern continued in operation until about 1980. ***Mulligans Too*** then operated from the site in the early 1980s. 58 Ocean Street is now home to ***Edward Jones Investments***.

Around 1936, Harry Silverman operated the ***Eagle Café*** at 53 Ocean Street; Silverman was also operating Joe's Cash Market across the street at the same time. Around 1937, Michael Keough operated ***Charlie's Café*** at 53 Ocean.

While 52 Ocean Street had formerly been a residence, restaurant activity started at the site in the 1930s. Elmer Harmon opened ***Harmon's Café*** around 1931. That was followed by ***French's Lunch***, run by William French from around 1932 to 1935. About 1937, Mrs. Sadie Brown operated a restaurant known as the ***Nite-Ville Café***. ***Mack's Café*** ran from about 1938 to 1941, operated by Mrs. Gladys MacKenzie. Then Mrs. Mary Whitmore operated ***Mary's Lunch*** around 1942-1943.

Around 1945, the ***Shangri-La Café*** opened. This café was run for many years by Alexander Seader III. Seader closed the business around 1960 and opened The 707 Restaurant just up the street. The site at 52 Ocean was later used for many years by the Red Cab Company.

Betty McGonigle and Lillian Whitmore in front of the Shangri-La, 52 Ocean
Courtesy of David Soule

Now site of a new professional medical building, home to **Bowdoin Medical Group**, 51 Ocean Street was formerly a gas station and residential apartments in the late 1920s and 1930s.

Around 1938, **Sam's Open Air Market** and **Coleman E. Donahue Restaurant** opened at the site. Donahue's quickly closed and Sam's Open Air Market only operated for a few years. Later businesses included William's Auto Sales, Curley's Used Cars, Traders Antiques and Morrill's Decorator Shop. Around 1962, a new building was constructed and **Ocean Street Car Wash** would then occupy that corner into the 1990s.

Morrill's Decorator Shop at 51 Ocean Street in the late 1950s. Bowdoin Medical Group now operates from a new professional building on the site.
Courtesy of South Portland Public Library

As mentioned previously, **Mooradian Bros.** operated a grocery from 50 Ocean Street from the late 1920s to mid-1930s. Around 1935-1936, **Joe's Cash Market** was in business, run by Harry Silverman and Simon Zeitman. George Levine then opened **George's Market** at the site around 1937, but that store soon closed.

From around 1929 to 1934, Robert Smith operated **Smith's Lunch** at 48 Ocean Street. Henry Alix ran **Henry's Café** here around 1935; the following year, Alix moved his café to 112 Ocean Street. Alix had previously run Henry's Café at 46 Ocean Street around 1940.

The **Nite-Ville Café**, run by Frank Berry, was located at 48 Ocean Street around 1936, followed by **Hank's Place,** a restaurant run by Henry Klenke around 1937. Around 1940, *The Fish Market* operated for a short time. In the 1940s, the site was home to *Paradise Cleansers & Dyers* and then *Ideal Cleaners*.

60 Minute Photo was established in Mill Creek in 1983 and had moved to this 37 Ocean Street address in 1985. The building has undergone a sizeable expansion compared to this 1989 view.

Courtesy of Bill Ciccarone

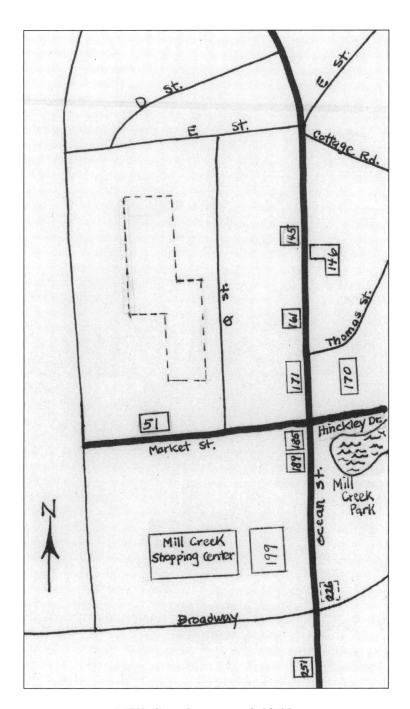

Mill Creek around 1960*
(*former and later stores with dashed lines)

Six

Mill Creek

For the past 50 years, Mill Creek has grown to be the shopping center for many South Portland and Cape Elizabeth residents. What a transformation the Mill Creek Park has seen - the site was formerly the city dump!

With the opening of the Shaw's "super" market on Ocean Street in 1951, and then the Mill Creek Shopping Center in 1955, Mill Creek set the stage for a major change in shopping habits of South Portland residents. It is easy to look at the development of Mill Creek and in it, see the dividing line between the way shopping "used to be" and what it is today. No longer would customers head to their corner grocery and be waited on by a store clerk. The entire shopping experience had moved into a new era.

Johnson's Pharmacy at 145 Ocean Street.

Courtesy of the City of South Portland

Johnson's Pharmacy was established at 145 Ocean Street in the 1920s by Thomas Johnson. His son, George Johnson, later took over the pharmacy. The business closed after George Johnson's death in August 1965. ***Richard's Discount Beauty Shop***, and later ***Jeannie's Hair Fashions***, operated from this site until 1972 when Glenice and James Hodgson bought it and established ***Glenice's Hair Fashions***. Although under different ownership, Glenice's continues in business today.

The companies conducting business from 146 Ocean Street have ranged from undertakers to driving schools. At the turn of the century, ***Clarence E. Turner*** ran his blacksmith shop from the site.

Turner's Blacksmith Shop at 146 Ocean Street in the early 1900s
Courtesy of the South Portland Historical Society

Turner operated his blacksmith shop from the site into the early 1920s, then *I. Howard Harriman, Blacksmith* and *S. King Starbird, Undertaker* were in business in the 1920s. *Henry Boland* ran his Ford sales and service operation from 146 Ocean Street in the 1930s through 1950s. Other businesses have included *Percival's Appliance & Kitchen Center*, *The Pop Shoppe*, *Genuine Auto Parts*, *Big Red Q QuickPrint*, *Colonial Cleaners* and *Ocean Fitness*. Bob Boylen's State Farm insurance office is now at the site, as well as the Best-Way Driving School.

The Pop Shoppe opened at 146 Ocean Street in 1976 and operated for several years. The store offered a variety of flavored sodas in small bottles. The Pop Shoppe was ahead of its time as it offered customers money back when they returned their bottles so the store could wash and reuse them.
Courtesy of Darrell and Martha Johnston

The ***South Portland Filling Station*** was a long-running service station, owned and operated by the Prout family. According to H. Rockwell Prout, his grandfather Charles H. Prout first started South Portland Filling Station in 1924 at 225 Ocean Street. The business moved to 161 Ocean Street around the early 1930s. The service station remained at this location until around 1953. The Prouts then opened a new service station at 585 Broadway and that station would continue to operate for several decades.

In this 1931 photo, South Portland Filling Station is shown at 161 Ocean Street. Johnson's Pharmacy can be seen on the far right.
Courtesy of the South Portland Historical Society

After the South Portland Filling Station closed at 161 Ocean Street, the building was closed and a grocery store was built. ***First National Stores*** operated from the site from 1954 to the late 1960s.

The First National Store on Ocean Street, between Uncle Andy's and Johnson's Pharmacy.
Courtesy of the Portland Press Herald

At a site formerly home to several service stations, the Great Atlantic & Pacific Tea Co. opened its *A&P* store at <u>47 Thomas Street</u> in the late 1930s. The store operated from that building until the early 1960s when a new store was built next to the original store and the address changed to <u>170 Ocean Street</u>. The A&P continued in operation here until the early 1970s.

The A&P Store at 170 Ocean Street. The site is now home to the Mill Creek Financial Center, which houses several businesses, including Blake, Hall & Allen and Town & Country Federal Credit Union.

Courtesy of the City of South Portland

Uncle Andy's Bakery was an institution at <u>171 Ocean Street</u>. In the late 1940s, Fred Nanney opened Uncle Andy's Donut Shop. Nanney hired John Palanza to run the operation and by 1951, Palanza had bought the business. He and his wife, Helen, ran Uncle Andy's Bakery as a family business for decades; indeed, the bakery was a fixture in Mill Creek for half a century.

John Palanza (right) was no ordinary baker. He was truly an artist, creating exquisite and unusual cakes. One of his truly amazing accomplishments came in 1954, when he created a 750-pound cake in the shape of a Maine lobster, complete with legs, claws and feelers. This edible lobster cake was frosted with 150 pounds of bright red frosting. Other notable cakes which he and his talented employees made over the years included replicas of the Prince of Fundy cruise ship, the Coast Guard station, the Maine Air National Guard building, the SP Police Station, and Jordan Marsh, as well as a birthday cake for President Carter.

Courtesy of John Palanza

Uncle Andy's Bakery at 171 Ocean Street   *Courtesy of John Palanza*

Although Uncle Andy's started out as a small doughnut shop, Palanza continually added new items to the product line over the years and the business grew. At one point, the bakery carried over 100 different freshly-baked items, including doughnuts, pies, turnovers, pastries, breads, muffins, and cookies.

While John Palanza devoted most of his time to the baking and "back of the house" activities, his wife, Helen (*shown at left*) was the constant presence in the front of the shop, always serving customers with a smile. It was a true family operation, with siblings, children, spouses, nieces, nephews, neighbors and even their grandson, all working there over the years.

Courtesy of John Palanza

The picture at right shows their son, Billy standing next to an Uncle Andy's delivery truck. The bakery's employees were also considered family to the Palanzas. The employees were hard-working, loyal and very talented. It was a fun, happy atmosphere.

Courtesy of John Palanza

Uncle Andy's Bakery maintained strong community ties throughout its operation, offering employment for local high school students, and food donations to churches, schools, shelters, food pantries, and festivals.

John Palanza retired from the bakery in October 1992, and Helen stayed on in the operation until her sudden death in August 1993. The business was then sold to one of their employees.

It was a sad day for South Portland when Uncle Andy's Bakery closed its doors in March 1998. In today's whole-grain, carb-conscious world, most bakeries of this style have also closed. The picture at left showing the cases of cookies, cream-filled pastries and other treats is a rare sight today.

Courtesy of John Palanza

At 173 Ocean Street, in the house next to Uncle Andy's, there was a pinball parlor in the mid-1950s. The local kids called the place **Ma's Pinball Parlor**. There were no signs outside; word of mouth was all that was needed. Mary McDonough ran the place, serving hot dogs, hamburgers, chips and soda out of the kitchen. In the late 1950s, Mary's sons, Alfred and Richard McDonough ran the Chuck Wagon at 791 Broadway. Alfred McDonough's specialty was clam cakes, and he would make them at Ma's Pinball Parlor as well.

This 1951 photo shows Shaw's as a stand-alone store. The buildings to the right housed a diner and a doughnut shop at 185 and 189 Ocean Street.
Courtesy of the South Portland Historical Society

A diner was located at <u>185 Ocean Street</u>. In the late 1930s and through World War II, George Curtis ran **Pop's Lunch**. After the war, the **Park View Restaurant** was operating from the building, then **Bob's Diner** in the early 1950s. In 1953, a new building was built at 185 Ocean to house **Henry J. Boland** auto dealer. That building was the future home of **Hodges Furniture** and Appliances, and now houses a Naval recruiting office, **Papa John's Pizza**, and **Curves Fitness Center**.

At <u>189 Ocean Street</u>, during the early-to-mid-1950s, the **Do-Nut Hole** was in operation. Resident Mike Eastman remembers going into the doughnut shop and seeing a sign hanging on the wall that read, "Wherever you may wander, whatever be your goal, keep your eye upon the doughnut, and be sure it's Do-Nut Hole".

According to H. Rockwell Prout, his grandfather Charles H. Prout started the **South Portland Filling Station** at <u>225 Ocean Street</u> in 1924. The station was a family-run operation and was sold to Gulf Oil in the early 1930s. South Portland Filling Station then moved to 161 Ocean, and later to 585 Broadway. After Gulf Oil bought the station, there were at least nine other operators of the station before it was finally left vacant in the late 1960s. In 1969, John Angelone established **Angelone's Pizza** on that corner.

Most residents may not realize that there once was a store at <u>226 Ocean Street</u>, on the corner of Broadway and Ocean. The building sat on the corner of what would later become Mill Creek Park. The park itself was originally the site of the city dump, and the school on the other side of Broadway provided a steady supply of customers.

Looking out from the school window, The Corner Store (formerly Buchanan's) can be seen on the far corner (look behind the students lined up outside, just below the center point of the photo). The little white building was run by Harold F. Buchanan from the mid-1920s to the mid-1930s, then Mrs. Elinor McFarland took over the store and ran it until the early 1940s.

Courtesy of the City of South Portland

In the years that The Corner Store was in operation, South Portland High School was located on the other side of Broadway (what is now Mahoney Middle School on Ocean Street). In the 1927 yearbook, **Buchanan's** advertised its hot dogs, soft drinks, candy, cigars and tobacco. In the 1929 yearbook, their advertisement read "Buchanan's Hot Dogs, necessary for any senior to graduate." South Portland High School alum Bob Dunlop remembers the store when he was at the high school, around 1939 to 1941. He recalls how Mrs. McFarland would break open packs of cigarettes so that customers could buy just one. By 1942, the store had closed and by 1944, the building was gone.

Later in the 1940s, **Bagley's Variety Store** opened across from the high school at 251 Ocean Street. The little candy store run by Harold Bagley was well attended by area students. Bagley was legally blind and some residents remember him listening to the sounds of coins as they hit the counter. When it came to paper money, Bagley's young patrons were sure to watch and make sure that no one took advantage of their beloved shopkeeper. According to resident Scott Robinson, "All the boys met at Bagley's." Any poor soul who attempted to fool Mr. Bagley would not have much luck with everyone watching out. Another resident, Barry Edwards says of Mr. Bagley: "He was so nice to everybody. He was such a nice man. He'd let you hang out as long as you behaved…kids would help him stock shelves." Edwards remembers the Ring Dings and Casco sodas for sale. The store also carried cigarettes.

Bagley's Variety ran for nearly three decades. After it closed in the mid-1970s, the store remained vacant for a short time, and then **Helen Rediker Hair Styling** opened. The building now houses **Madison Square Beauty Salon**.

The 1950s and 1960s were decades of incredible change in retail shopping habits, in South Portland as well as across the country. One of the early signs of this change in South Portland came in February 1951, when *Geo. C. Shaw Co.* opened a supermarket at 199 Ocean Street. The grand opening of the supermarket was highly publicized, with "Aunt Jemima" making a featured appearance to draw in the crowds. The store was referred to as "futuristic" when it opened, and the self-service style of shopping was called both convenient and economical.

This first Shaw's was a stand-alone building, sitting roughly where CVS is located in Mill Creek today. The opening of Shaw's and the subsequent construction of the Mill Creek Shopping Plaza was the beginning of the end for the small neighborhood grocer. The Mill Creek Shopping Plaza was a "one-stop shopping" area which encouraged residents to drive away from their neighborhoods to enjoy all the benefits of these clustered stores.

This 1955 photo shows the original Shaw's building in its stand alone building at 199 Ocean Street, as well as the new Mill Creek Shopping Center in a separate building. Henry J. Boland autos is at 185 Ocean Street and the building next door at 189 Ocean Street houses the Do-Nut Hole doughnut shop. Notice the large field on the other side of Market Street. In earlier times, this field was one of several locations in South Portland that was occasionally used for circus performances. The area is now paved over and is home to the Shaw's Millcreek Plaza.

Courtesy of the South Portland Historical Society

The Mill Creek Shopping Center is believed to be the first strip shopping center in Maine. This 1955 photo shows some of the early tenants after the shopping center had first opened: Shopper's Hardware, State of Maine Liquor Store, Slade's Shoe Center, Watkins Laundry Service, and Maine Savings Bank.   Courtesy of the Portland Press Herald

This 1961 photo shows the newly constructed Shaw's Supermarket on the other end of the Mill Creek Shopping Center, where Shopper's Hardware, Movie Gallery and Bank of America are today. Shaw's opened its 26,000 square foot store here in May 1961 and remained here for nearly three decades, moving across the street to the Mill Creek Plaza in October 1990.
Courtesy of the Portland Press Herald

In this 1960s photo, Shaw's has now moved to the other side of Mill Creek Shopping Center and the old Shaw's building is now occupied by Wellwood's. Notice how the old Shaw's building had been attached to the rest of the Shopping Center by an addition in the space between. The Bowl-A-Rama is at the top center of the photo.

Courtesy of the South Portland Historical Society

Wellwood's, shown here in a 1982 photo, was a wonderful department store in the Mill Creek Shopping Center. The store also featured a lunch counter. Resident Helen Macomber remembers a big draw of the lunch counter at Wellwood's: "Dottie Skillings' muffins - her muffins were famous."

Courtesy of Portland Press Herald

Resident Barbara Perry remembers Christmastime at Wellwood's. She and her husband had five children. "I would sit with some of the kids at the counter," she says. "A few of the kids would go around with their father to buy Christmas presents for me."

In this photo from June 1967, gasoline was only 28.9 cents a gallon at the little Top Gas filling station. The Bowl-A-Rama can be seen just beyond the gas station.   Courtesy of the City of South Portland

The Bowl-A-Rama in Mill Creek   Author's collection

The building at 51 Market Street which is now occupied by **Rite Aid** and the **Asia Restaurant**, originally was built as the **Bowl-A-Rama**. A candlepin bowling alley, it was in operation from roughly 1960 to 1980. There were also three pinball machines inside. One resident remembers being a teen in the early 1970s, playing the "Pinball Wizard" pinball machine, while Elton John's version of "Pinball Wizard" was playing in the bowling alley.

After the Bowl-A-Rama had ceased operations, a number of businesses operated from the site. First, **Eagle Savings & Loan** opened in the early 1980s. Then, by 1983, the building had been divided up and several businesses were running there at the same time. In the mid-1980s, the storefronts from left to right were **60 Minute Photo, Carvel Ice Cream,** and **Wellby Super Drug.** On the right side of the building, in the back, was **Gloria Stevens Figure Salon.**

The Gloria Stevens Figure Salon later became the China Dragon restaurant, and now houses the Asia Restaurant. The multiple storefronts in the front of the building have since been combined into one large space, now occupied by Rite Aid.

This circa 1983 photo shows Carvel Ice Cream in the middle storefront at 51 Market Street.

Courtesy of Bill Ciccarone

60 Minute Photo opens at 51 Market Street in the summer of 1984.
Courtesy of Bill Ciccarone

What is now Shaw's Plaza on Waterman Drive was built in the early 1970s. For the first two decades of its existence, the plaza was anchored by a large department store, allowing residents to shop for everything from clothing and toys, to gift wrap and sewing supplies. The first anchor store to open was the **Giant Department Store**. Giant operated for a few years, and **King's Department Store** opened around 1973.

In this 1983 photo, King's department store was about to close.
Courtesy of the Portland Press Herald

After the demise of King's in the early 1980s, **Mars** operated from the space from the mid-to-late-1980s. After Mars closed, the building was vacant for a short time. Then in the early 1990s, the building was renovated and **Shaw's Supermarket,** which had been operating across the street in the Mill Creek Plaza, moved to its current site.

The **Carriage Lantern** was one of the original stores in the plaza, and continues in operation today. One of the other original stores was **Russell's** clothing store.

In this 1990 photograph, Mars department store had closed and Shaw's was soon to renovate the space into a large full-service supermarket.

Courtesy of the City of South Portland

In the parking lot of the (then) Mars Plaza, Fotomat was a small drive-up booth for photo developing, from the mid-to-late-1980s.

Courtesy of the City of South Portland

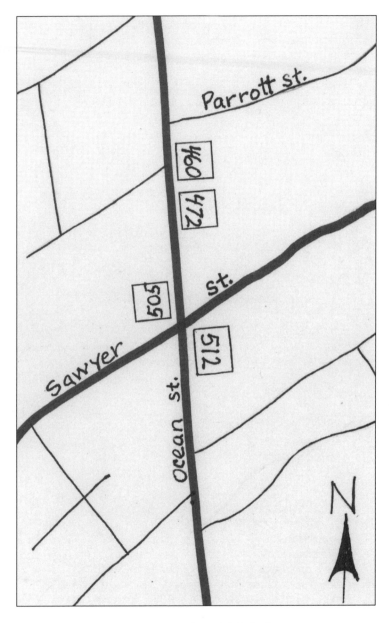

South Portland Heights

Seven

South Portland Heights

At the turn of the 20th century, this neighborhood was referred to as Town House Corner, as the town hall and school were located in a building where Hamlin School now stands. Over the years, residents began referring to the area as South Portland Heights; from atop Parrott Street, one can easily see why it took on that name, as there is a nice view of Portland from the top of the hill.

The retail center of South Portland Heights is located at the intersection of Sawyer and Ocean Streets, with a few buildings running down Ocean Street that have housed many storefronts over the years. As traffic there has increased, so has the feel of the intersection. Resident Frances Heller remembers the days when she would play "kick the can" in the middle of the intersection.

Franklin W. Dyer operated this market at <u>516 Ocean Street</u> in the 1890s. Along with running this general store, he was also listed as a market gardener at 499 Ocean. The store remained in operation until Dyer's death in 1915. In the late 1910s, Frank C. Sawyer ran the store, then moved the business to 460 Ocean Street around 1920. Frank Sawyer had previously run a meat/grocery business at the corner of Broadway and Evans Street in Pleasantdale.
From the antique post card collection of John and Patti Vierra, Gray, Maine

Next to F.W. Dyer's store, on the corner of Sawyer and Ocean, 512 Ocean Street was originally home to a blacksmith and carriage painting business operated by **Otis Hannaford** in the 1800s. By 1895, **Dyer and Jose** was a grocery and post office at the site. Operated by C. Fremont Jose (the name is pronounced "Joce") and Howard Dyer, the business thrived. After ten years in business, Dyer sold his interest to Jose, who ran the store until the late 1910s.

Dyer & Jose Grocers at 512 Ocean at the turn of the century. *R.C. Craig photo*

Around 1918, **Harry D. Lord** bought the business at 512 Ocean and ran the grocery until the early 1920s. Harry Lord was a professional baseball player who started out his major-league career playing third base for the Boston Americans in 1907. He played for the Boston Red Sox from 1908 to 1910, the Chicago White Sox from 1910 to 1914, and the Buffalo Buffeds in 1915 – his last year in the big league.

Around 1923, **George Lang** took over the business. His store became affiliated with IGA in the 1930s and Lang ran the store for almost two decades, closing it around the start of World War II. The store remained vacant for a year or so, and then **Leon Johnson** ran the store through the remainder of the war.

Ralph Haskell opened **Haskell's Nation Wide** around 1946 and continued running that store until about 1963 when he moved his grocery to 124 Sawyer Street in Ferry Village. In the mid-1960s, Harry McMann briefly operated the **Corner Market**, and then the store was acquired by Bill and Lucy Stanton.

According to the Stantons' son, Jeff, his family grew up on Ocean Street. Both Bill and Lucy had previous food experience. In 1965, the Stantons bought the store, moved in upstairs and opened **Patty Ann's**. Lucy Stanton ran the store, while Bill kept his job as a bartender at Portland Country Club and helped in the store on weekends. Patty Ann's was a real family operation. The Stantons' daughter, Patty Ann worked in the store, and the Stanton boys helped out also.

When Patty Ann's was first open, the store was set up as a full-line grocery store, but as the larger supermarkets opened and the Stantons saw the change in their customers' buying habits, they wisely changed the product line and transitioned into more of a variety/convenience store, selling primarily sandwiches, pizza, chips, bread and milk. As a corner store, it became a gathering place for the kids in the neighborhood.

Patty Ann's Deli at 512 Ocean Street in 1983.   *Courtesy of Jeff Stanton*

In 1983, the Stantons sold the business to Dennis and Mary Lou Gentilini. According to the Gentilinis' son Matt, they left the Patty Ann's name on the store for a few years, and then changed the name to ***Lighthouse Deli.*** The store offered a huge wine selection; according to Matt Gentilini, it was one of the biggest in the state at that time.

The Gentilinis sold the business in the early 1990s to Jack Moran, who ran ***Lighthouse Deli & Wine Cellar*** for a few years, then closed it. It remained vacant until the late 1990s when Steven and Claudia DiCicco bought it and established ***DiCicco's Deli and Groceria***, selling gourmet sandwiches and take-home dinners. In 2004, Claude Francke bought the business and changed the name back to the ***Lighthouse Deli***.

At <u>505 Ocean Street</u>, on the opposite corner of Sawyer and Ocean, ***Dennison's Pharmacy*** was in operation for over 30 years.

During World War II, Keith Dennison, Sr. (*left*) worked in the shipyards. A forward-thinker, he saved his money and after the war bought the small apple orchard on the corner of Occan and Sawyer Streets. Along with help from family and friends, Dennison built the building himself and opened Dennison's Pharmacy on April 15, 1946.

Courtesy of Keith Dennison, Jr.

Dennison's Pharmacy offered prescription services and cosmetics, along with a soda fountain, sundaes, milkshakes, and Russell Stover chocolates. The original one-story building housed the pharmacy on the left side; on the right side of the building, there was a beauty shop in front and a barbershop in back.

Dennison's Pharmacy at 505 Ocean Street.   *Courtesy of Keith Dennison, Jr.*

As the pharmacy business grew over the next few years, the barbershop became **The Toggery** (a clothing store) and eventually Dennison would add a second story to the structure.

After Dennison's death in 1955, his son, Keith Dennison, Jr. *(right)* took over and ran the business. The pharmacy continued to grow, reaching its peak after some of the other local pharmacies closed (Anderson's Pharmacy, Willard Square Pharmacy, Johnson's Pharmacy) and sold their prescriptions to Dennison's. In 1979, Dennison's Pharmacy merged with Mill Creek Pharmacy. Sea Rose interior design is now located in the building.

Courtesy of Keith Dennison, Jr

Public Works employees are painting a crosswalk on Ocean Street. The two-story Dennison's Pharmacy building is in the background.

Courtesy of the City of South Portland

To the right of Dennison's Pharmacy at 503 Ocean was Ruby's Beauty Salon, operated by Ruby Hitchcock. A sign on the tree at right advertises The Toggery Shop which was run from the back of the building at the time of this early photo. The Toggery was a retail clothing store, selling men's and boys' clothing. William R. Smith was the proprietor.

Courtesy of Keith Dennison, Jr.

A little further down Ocean Street on the right are two store buildings with a lot of history. At 472 Ocean Street, there is a very large building with multiple storefronts today. In years past, there was another building attached to the right-hand side of 472 Ocean. The address was 474 Ocean and that building was home to *James A. Fullum, Blacksmith* in the the early 1900s through the 1920s. In the 1930s, Robert Horne Auto Repairing was operating.

One of the longest running businesses at 472 Ocean Street was the *Ocean Street Garage*, run by Herbert Davis from the 1950s to 1980s. Other occupants over the years include *Ocean House Fish Market,* The Hair Force, Off the Wall Antiques, *The Maine Seafood Company, Cream of the Crop Consignment Shop,* Belissimo and Kim's Alterations.

In the early 1920s, *Frank C. Sawyer* moved his grocery from 516 Ocean Street to 460 Ocean Street, in a building just to the left of the old blacksmith shop. Around 1923, *John H. Crouchen* took over the store and started his own grocery.

Resident Frances Heller remembers the big wooden pickle barrel, full of brine in Johnny Crouchen's store. The charge was 5 cents for a pickle. Crouchen, who lived upstairs, would use a big spoon to scoop out the pickles. Heller also remembers buying milk in the store for 15 cents a quart, and five penny candies for one penny. "My uncle would give us two pennies, to go to the store and buy him a cigar," she says. Johnny Crouchen's store was in operation through the mid-1940s, then *Owen Pride* bought the store and ran it until the early 1950s.

Curtis and Georgietta Bunker established their *Market Basket* store in the early 1950s. After Curtis' death in August 1954, his wife Georgietta continued operating the market until about 1960. Gerard O'Neill then took over the Market Basket and ran the store for several years, until selling the business to Harry and Maria Koukos in the mid-1960s.

Under Harry and Maria Koukos' ownership, the *Market Basket* was a real family business, serving great Italian sandwiches, soda, chips, beer, wine, and other grocery-type items for nearly 40 years. Harry Koukos had previously owned and operated a store in Portland, and had worked at the Broadway Market for a few years before establishing this store. "Everyone called it 'Harry's'," remembers Angie Koukos, Harry's son. "We had six kids in the family and we all worked there as kids."

In 1985, Angie and his brother, Louie took over the business; they continued to operate the store for another 17 years, selling the business in the early 2000s. The store continued in operation under new owners for a few years, before closing in the spring of 2004. The space is now occupied by *Fleur de Lis.*

Harry and Maria Koukos standing in front of their long-running, much loved Harry's Market Basket store.   *Photos courtesy of the Koukos family*

Harry Koukos with his son Louie in front of the store.

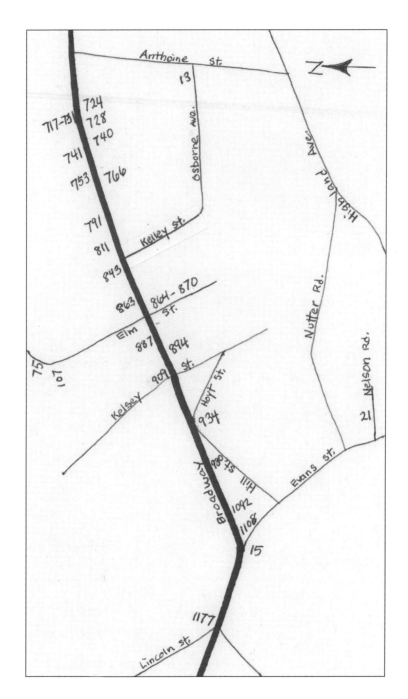

Pleasantdale

Eight

Pleasantdale

The area now known as Pleasantdale has its roots in two separate sections of early Cape Elizabeth: Turner's Island (heading down Elm Street toward the Fore River) and Cape Elizabeth Depot (near the intersection of Broadway with Evans Street). Over time, the name Pleasantdale became used to identify the entire area and at one point, Pleasantdale even loosely covered the area up towards the present-day high school, Highland Avenue and Stanwood Park. Once the tank farm went in, between Kelsey Street and Nutter Road, the high school area became somewhat isolated from the rest of Pleasantdale, and so Pleasantdale is rarely given such a broad definition any longer.

Many older Pleasantdale inhabitants have fond memories of the way Elm Street used to be. As one can imagine, the street got its name from the beautiful elm trees that once lined the roadway. As with many other areas in Maine, however, the elm trees were lost to Dutch Elm disease.

Starting at 13 Osborne Avenue, off Anthoine Street, the origin of the *Osborne Avenue Market*, dates back to the 1920s when *William H. Sweet* ran a small grocery at 70 Anthoine Street. In the mid '20s, Sweet moved his grocery business to 6 Columbus Avenue, then to 8 Osborne Avenue in the late 1920s, and finally to 13 Osborne Avenue in the early 1930s. During World War II, *Norman Smith* ran the business for a short time, and then the market closed for a year, and reopened toward the end of the war under the name *Sweet's Market*. After just a few years as Sweet's, *K.H. Burns* ran the store around 1947, and then the name officially became Osborne Avenue Market around 1948. At first, Charles LaVallee was listed as the store's proprietor. Lynwood Whitney took over the store in the 1960s.

Local resident Barbara Perry remembers the store. "One of my sons loved to get the pickles. He [Mr. Whitney] had a pickle barrel in the store," she says. Her children also remember going to the counter in the back corner of the store, where they could buy bologna, salt pork, and cheese. The store carried various staples, such as bread, milk, and other groceries, plus penny candy for the kids. There was an apartment over the store, which Mr. Whitney rented out to tenants. After the store was sold in the early 1970s, the building was converted to a residence.

In the general area of the current *Thomas Room*, the *Jack-O-Lantern Dancing Pavilion* once stood at 717-731 Broadway from the mid-1920s to the late 1940s. Around 1950, the building had been converted to *The Jack Roller Skating Rink,* and then was changed back to the Jack-O-Lantern Dance Pavilion for a few years. By the mid-1950s, the roller skating rink was being run by Myer Simon and was known as *Roll-A-Way Skating Rink.*

Shoppers Mart Discount Dept. Store, formerly Jack-O-Lantern dance pavilion
Collections of Maine Historical Society

In September 1956, the new **Shoppers Mart Discount Department Store** opened at 717-731 Broadway. Shoppers Mart sold clothing and shoes for adults and children. In the 1960s, the city turned down a proposal to join the Shoppers Mart and Fantastic Fair buildings (to make one large sales floor). The Shoppers Mart site was then leased to Applicators Sales & Service.

Shoppers Mart and Twin City Discount on Broadway
Courtesy of the City of South Portland

In the late 1950s, the **Twin City Discount** store opened at <u>741 Broadway</u>, to the left of Shoppers Mart. At <u>753 Broadway</u>, Philip R. Yerxa Fuel Oil was already in operation. Although 741 and 753 are different addresses, it was one large building and a person could walk through Yerxa's to reach the department store.

In the early 1960s, ***Fantastic Fair Department Store*** took over the space previously occupied by Twin City. Then in the mid-1960s, the ***Globe Discount Department Store*** took over the business.

Like the other department stores, the Globe sold a wide variety of items. Resident Karen Harvey remembers going to the Globe to buy toys and 45's (to the younger readers: 45's were vinyl disks, otherwise known as "records").

After the Globe closed in the early 1970s, ***Yerxa's Garden Center*** moved into the building from its former location across the street.

In the early 1940s, Freemont B. Suddy operated ***Suddy's Restaurant*** at 724 Broadway. He had already been operating ***Suddy's Service Station*** next door at 728 Broadway since the mid-1930s. Around 1943, Suddy moved down to run the Whitehall facility at 894 Broadway, and Althea Bachelder began running the business, changing the name to ***Ma's Place***. The restaurant was closed shortly thereafter, but the service station continued at 728 Broadway, along with a variety store. In the early 1950s, Mrs. Bachelder closed the service station, and the variety store's name changed from Ma's Place to ***Rainbow Variety***.

One of Althea (Palmer) Bachelder's beloved dogs in front of Ma's Place
Courtesy of the Palmer family

According to Steven Palmer, his great aunt "Lainey" (Althea Bachelder) was very fond of dogs. In the early 1950s, she had a shepherd and took it to dog shows. In the mid-1960s, Mrs. Bachelder would close her Rainbow Variety store and go on to open *Mill Creek Kennels*. South Portland resident David Soule remembers his family buying a poodle from Mrs. Bachelder in those days.

After Mill Creek Kennels closed a few years later, the building remained vacant into the early 1970s. Subsequent businesses which operated from the building include Ronnie's Color TV Service, Ken & Babe's Browse Shoppe and then *Mickey's Sandwich Shop* in the early 1980s.

Yerxa's Garden Center was originally established at 740 Broadway. Yerxa's operated here in the 1960s and early 1970s before moving across the street to its present location at 753 Broadway in the early 1970s. *Newick's Seafood Restaurant* opened in the mid-1970s, originally known as *Cap'n Newick's Lobster House*.

The *House of Hay* operated from the location at 766 Broadway from the mid-1960s until around 1970. It is remembered by some local residents as a type of breakfast/coffee shop. Resident Helen Macomber remembers it as a very small place with a little counter and three or four stools. After the House of Hay closed, *Kentucky Fried Chicken* opened in the space and ran for about a decade. Other businesses at the site have included *Broadway Meat Market*, *Broadway Redemption Center* and now Neighborhood Laundromat.

There were a number of service stations in operation at 791 Broadway during the decades prior to the 1950s. In the 1950s, *Shaw's Doughnut Shop* was run for a short time by Vincent Shaw; it was primarily a wholesale business, but customers could walk in and buy the doughnuts retail.

The *Chuck Wagon* was in operation at 791 Broadway in the late 1950s. Alfred McDonough opened the Chuck Wagon with his brother Richard. The Chuck Wagon was a little take-out shop, selling clams, clam cakes, sodas, and featuring their tenderloin steak sandwich. According to McDonough, the business also offered catering services, which his brother Richard handled. Alfred's specialty was his clam cakes.

After the Chuck Wagon closed, Continental Baking Co. operated from the site from the early to mid-1960s, and then Charles Redstone and Frank Keenan opened *Charlie and Frank's Variety Store* around 1967. The store sold the standard variety staples of bread, milk, soda, and other groceries, and was known for its Italian sandwiches. In the later years of its existence, the store was run by Charlie and his wife, Fran.

Charlie and Frank's closed around 1974, and then *Booth's Variety*, run by Howard Booth, operated from the building for a short time.

Kenneth and Joan Whitmore started *Mid-Town Market* at 791 Broadway around 1975 and ran the store for 10 years. Ken Whitmore had previously worked as a radio broadcaster and news director for WCSH for many years. Despite the lack of experience, Ken and Joan "Mama Mid-Town" Whitmore worked hard and built a thriving business. They had a few employees, but it was mostly family working in the store: Ken, Joan and their three children. Along with the usual milk, bread, beer, soda, chips and cigarettes, Mid-Town Market offered red hot dogs, pizza and Italian sandwiches.

Ken and Joan Whitmore inside their Mid-Town Market at 791 Broadway

Photos courtesy of Karen Harvey

The sandwich business grew over the years, with the store becoming known for its steak sandwiches. Mr. Whitmore would buy whole roasts and slice them for the freshest steak sandwiches, prepared with the Whitmores' own "secret sauce". The meatball sandwiches were made with Joan's homemade meatballs. As time went on, the sandwiches were given names like "The Bomb," "The Atomic Bomb" and "The Roast Beef Riot."

After the Mid-Town Market closed, no other store opened in the space. The building was later torn down and the footprint of the building now lies roughly in the parking lot of the Greater Portland Municipal Credit Union.

At 811 Broadway, *Harry E. Morse* ran a grocery store from the mid-1920s to the mid-1930s. The market was taken over by *Lawrence J. McCabe* around 1938. McCabe had previously run a grocery in Knightville at 62 Ocean Street. McCabe ran his grocery at 811 Broadway until around 1947 when *Virgie Moutsatsos* took over. The grocery then had a quick progression of owners: *John Paulsen* around 1949, *Aceto's Groceries* around 1950, and then Evangeline Dow ran *Vange's Dining Room* around 1951. By 1952, the storefront was vacated.

At 843 Broadway, Thomas Carmody opened a small ice cream shop with his brother-in-law in the late 1940s, known as *Tom's Ice Cream Shop.* There was no seating, but customers could walk in and order Tom's homemade ice cream. The business was only in operation for about one year. Thomas Carmody was also a South Portland police officer and would later go on to run The Dory on Willard Beach with his wife, Alice.

On Broadway near Elm Street, this 1950s photo shows the Pleasantdale Red & White Store on the left, run by Wally Demmons, and the Broadway Pharmacy on the right.

Courtesy of the City of South Portland

At 863 Broadway, near the intersection of Broadway and Elm, was the *Pleasantdale Red & White Store,* originally operated by Frank W. "Wally" Demmons. Demmons had previously operated this Red & White across the street at 866 Broadway, and moved the business to this location in the late

1940s. After the Red & White closed in the early 1960s, the ***Pleasantdale Superette*** operated from the building for several years, run by Steve Christie (formerly a partner in Nanos Grocery). Scott Macomber remembers when Steve Christie was running the store. There was a fruit stand outside and bananas were a penny apiece.

In 1965, Tony DiMillo leased the store, calling it ***T's Variety***. DiMillo, who later founded DiMillo's Floating Restaurant in Portland, ran the store for about a year, then sold the business to Peter Field. In the latter part of the 1960s, an explosion and resulting fire gutted the building. The current ***House of Frames*** began operation there in 1969.

There has long been activity on the corner of Broadway and Elm Streets. In the early 1920s, pharmacist Clifford Ward moved the old building from the corner down a few store lengths and built a new building on the site, with the old building attached at the end. In that old building, the ***A&P*** operated (at 866 Broadway) through the 1920s and '30s. In the early 1930s, Millard C. Emery began managing the A&P; he continued running it through the early 1940s, established a ***Red & White Store*** there when the A&P closed, and by about 1942, the Red & White closed and Mr. Emery was listed as joining the Navy during World War II. The storefront remained vacant for a short time, then ***Frank "Wally" Demmons*** started a new grocery at 866 Broadway and by the late 1940s, he moved his grocery across the street and established the Pleasantdale Red & White Store there. When Demmons moved out of 866 Broadway, Ward's Drug Store expanded into the space.

In a little store to the left of the Red & White, at 864 Broadway, there were a multitude of shops over the years, including the following: ***Harry Bacon Barber Shop***, Sam's Radio Shop and Libby Novelty Company in the 1940s; ***Robert Stewart Barber Shop*** and ***George Howland Barber Shop*** in the 1950s; ***Pleasantdale Tailor Shop***, ***William Cloutier Barber Shop*** and ***Richard's Discount Beauty Salon*** in the 1960s; ***Al's Variety*** and ***Broadway Luncheonette*** in the 1970s; ***Luis Cidre's Shoe Repair Shop*** in the 1970s and '80s; and Shoestring Exchange Shoe Repair in the 1990s.

Back during the time when the A&P was operating, ***Blue Bird Stores*** was located in the storefront to its right in the late 1920s. Later businesses in that 868 Broadway storefront include ***Elaine's Beauty Salon***, Specialties of Maine, Town & Country Upholstery, A Furniture Find and ***The Drapery Trading Company***.

Ward's Drug Store and the Red & White Store, circa 1941.
Courtesy of Isabelle Williams

After Clifford Ward built the new building on the corner, he established **Ward's Drug Store** in the early 1920s at 870 Broadway. In the late 1940s, Ward expanded the store down into the storefront vacated by the Red & White. After Clifford Ward died, in the early 1950s Carl Graffam bought the store and renamed it **Broadway Pharmacy**.

Resident Helen Macomber remembers the drugstore when Carl Graffam and his wife, Velma were running the place. There was a lunch counter in the back of the store on the left where customers could sit and have a cup of coffee and a doughnut. The cash register was on the other side of the store, on the right side in front. The drugstore sold a little bit of everything, from prescriptions to clocks.

Cathy Counts, who grew up in the neighborhood, vividly remembers the store: "I remember going into the Rexall Pharmacy there when I was a little girl in the 1950s, and it was old then, with sagging, rolling, but highly polished dark wooden floors and elaborate molding on the columns, and high, ornate tin ceilings. I sat at the lunch counter and twirled on the seat while the proprietor heated my Heinz 57 Tomato Soup and grilled my cheese sandwich and topped off my lemon blend, for $1.10, every school day. Meanwhile the school teachers, also on their lunch breaks, smoked cigarettes, laughed and ate sandwiches a little ways down the long counter from where I whirled back and forth, the toes of my patent leather shoes scuffing a trail along the wooden paneling under the counter as I breezed by. Of course, we all wore dresses then, and the teachers all had their hair 'done'. My mother worked as a nurse, unlike all the other mothers in the neighborhood, who were home for their children at lunchtime. I felt quite worldly, the one child on her own at lunch, not Mothered."

Broadway Pharmacy continued in operation until around 1967. Around 1970, *L & A Variety* opened at 870 Broadway, run by Louis and Athena Germaine until the early 1980s. Later stores include *Shenanigan's Deli* and *The Corner Store* in the 1980s, *Black Tie Catering* in the 1990s and now *Diva Hair Studio*.

On another corner of Broadway and Elm, <u>875 Broadway</u> has seen its share of occupants, including the Elm Street School, Pleasantdale Hose Company, VFW, Knights of Columbus, the Moose Lodge, Bike & Blade Sports Center, and currently Big Red Q Quickprint and Cheryl Greeley Dance Studio.
Courtesy of the City of South Portland

Heading down Elm Street, approaching the turn onto Turner's Island, there was once a store on the left at <u>75 Elm Street</u>. Around 1919, *Sumner Shaw* was running a grocery there, then *Nellie Shaw* ran it from about 1920-1921. Around 1922, *Aaron Burnham* ran the store, then *Herbert Olds* around 1924, and *Frederick Taylor* from about 1925-1933. From around 1934 to the early 1940s, the store became the *Pleasantdale Market*. The last store to occupy 75 Elm Street was **King's Pleasantdale Market**, run by Gladys King in the late 1940s and through the 1950s.

*Above is an early, turn of the century photo of the Knapp Bros. grocery at **107 Elm Street**. Knapp Bros. was run by J. Calvin Knapp and C. Lewis Knapp in the 1890s and early 1900s. Around 1904, the grocery became Palmer & Wilson, then became Walter H. Knight from about 1905 to 1909, and then Eugene Treworgy ran the store around 1912. Starting in the 1920s, Frank T. Palmer began an auto service business there, later known as Elm Street Garage.*

Courtesy of Elm Street United Methodist Church, Hiram Blanchard photographer

Whitehall was established by William J. White in 1903 at 344 Summer Street (later renamed/numbered to <u>894 Broadway</u> in the 1920s). The very large three-story building housed a grocery store, a bowling alley, and a pool room. There was a large dance/meeting hall for the many dances that took place there over the years. The second and third floors were generally used for meetings of various local groups, including the Pleasantdale Grange.

Whitehall was run originally run by William White, then by Ernest L. Durost in the 1920s and 1930s. The Durosts lived upstairs. In the 1940s, Freemont B. Suddy ran the operation. A fire damaged the building in 1949 and although some rebuilding took place, the building was soon torn down and replaced by a service station. There have been many gas station/convenience stores there over the years, including Campbell's Pleasantdale Service Station, Cities Service Station, Canfield Oil Company, **Humphrey's Farm Stores,** **Red's Variety** and the **Big Apple**. Advantage Chiropractic now occupies the space.

Whitehall at 894 Broadway   *Courtesy of Isabelle Williams*

At 887 Broadway, across the street from Whitehall, a small grocery was in operation for many years. **Harold L. Sawyer** ran the grocery in the early 1920s, then **Frank J. Seeley** in the mid-1920s (Seeley went on to run a grocery at 185 Preble Street). In the late 1920s through mid-1930s, **Samuel E. Ireland** ran the store. **Harmon's Market** was open in the mid-1930s and **Your Market** in the late 1930s. Around the time of World War II, **Mrs. Park's Bakery** was in operation.

At 909 Broadway, where **Crest Glass** now stands on the corner of Kelsey Street, there previously was a very large building that was the largest grocery in Pleasantdale in the early days. At the beginning of the 1900s, **Ernest L. Sargent** was listed as the proprietor of the store, with William E. Dyer working there as a clerk. Dyer had previously operated his own small market on Evans Street in the 1890s. Will Dyer took over the store operation from Sargent, and went on to run the store for decades.

Will Dyer's Store had a large selection of items. Besides various canned goods, the store carried things like pickles, sugar, flour, and peanut butter in barrels, that would be scooped out as needed. Cookies and crackers were also sold by the pound. A butcher worked in a room toward the back of the store.

Around the end of World War II, **Malcolm G. MacLeod** is listed as taking over from Dyer. He would only run the store for about a year. Then, around 1947, James P. Boyd took over the business and changed the name to **Boyd's Market.**

Helen Macomber, a long-time Pleasantdale resident, recalls Mr. Boyd as a nice man who most locals referred to as "Boydie". "He had bins and bins of penny candy," she says. "The kids all stopped in on the way to school for a treat. They usually paid, but often they would sneak extra pieces. Boydie knew this, but he turned a blind eye because he loved all the kids. He loved to chat with his customers."

The building that Boyd's and Dyer's had occupied had been a large three-story structure, with wide steps across the front of the building. It would be a common sight in those days to see people relaxing on those steps.

In this 1968 photo, we can get a glimpse of what the old Dyer's/Boyd's building once looked like at 909 Broadway. A fire had gutted the Crest Glass building; a portion of the sign from the front of the building has fallen off, exposing letters from "Boyd's" underneath. After the fire, this building was torn down and a new building erected.   Courtesy of Tim Carr

Home to the long-running Campbell's Market, 934 Broadway has had a large number of grocers throughout the years. In the early years, **Eugene Roberts** ran a barber shop from the back of the building. Later, **Bob Stewart** ran his barber shop from the back.

William E. Bragdon ran his grocery store from the site from about 1918 to the late 1920s. During the 1920s, Bragdon was advertising fancy groceries, cigars, tobacco, soft drinks and ice cream for sale in his store.

Philip Hebert & Son operated in the early 1930s and by the mid-1930s, the name had changed to **Hebert's Market.** Other stores have included **Kittredge's Market** in the mid-to-late-1930s, **Joseph E. Landry** in the early-to-mid-1940s, **Noel's Market** in the late 1940s to early 1950s, **Tucker's Market** in the mid-1950s, and **Kern's Variety Store** around 1957.

In 1958, William Campbell established **Campbell's Market** at 934 Broadway. Campbell's Market remains one of the longest running family-owned stores in the city.

At 980 Broadway, now home to Domino's Pizza, the site started out around 1980 as an ice cream shop known as **Pic-It & Lic It.** Although Richard Montefesco continued to operate the shop until around 1984, the name changed to **Dick's Dairyland.** **Pat's Cozy Kitchen** operated at the site for a short time before **Domino's Pizza** took over the building in the mid-1980s.

The building at 1092 Broadway was originally a store run by **Lillian Cheney.** What a strong woman Lillian Cheney must have been. Born Lillian Richardson, she married Stanley Cheney in February 1909. Stanley died in 1912, leaving her with their two young children to support on her own. Mrs. Cheney purchased land at 1092 Broadway in April 1913 from Willard Fickett and had a house built. She raised her two children in the house, operating a small grocery from the front of the building.

According to Lillian Cheney's daughter, Dorothy Robinson, her mother "sold all the usual stuff of the day. She made pastries (cupcakes, etc.) and sold them in the store. Sometimes she would sell meat, she would buy a side of beef and cut it herself."

In January 1922, Lillian married Charles Fogg. They continued to live in the house, with Lillian running her store while Charles was employed in Portland. In February 1930, she sold the house and business, and she and Charles moved to Portland, where Lillian operated a lodginghouse after Charles died in 1932.

Alfred Murch bought the building and grocery from Lillian Fogg and went on to run his own small grocery from the 1930s until the mid-1950s.

While Alfred Murch was running his store from 1092 Broadway, Alfred Boudreau built a building next door at 1096 for his barber shop. In May 1954, Boudreau purchased the house/store from Alfred Murch, and renovated the space for a brand new hair salon, *House of Reau.* Cassiopeia Day Spa & Hair Salon was run from this building in the early 2000s. Then, Eclipse Hair & Nails began operation from the site in October 2002.

Lillian Cheney's store at 1092 Broadway in the 1910s. Lillian Cheney is on the left with her two children. Lillian's sister Laura is standing on the right with her daughter Ruth seated in front of her. Laura's husband had been a firefighter who had died in a Portland fire; Laura and her daughter lived in the house with Lillian and her kids. The old Summer Street/Reynolds School can be seen to the left of the store. The sign next to the door advertises "Cigars and Tobaccos, Stationery, Candies, Canned Goods". An interesting note in this picture: there is a swastika in the window. This store operated long before World War II occurred; in earlier times, the swastika was considered a good luck emblem.

Courtesy of Dorothy Robinson

At 1108 Broadway, on the corner of Broadway and Evans Street, have been a wide range of businesses over the years. Because of the way the house sat on the land, the original building (shown in the next photo) had a store operating out of the basement/first floor. The living quarters were up over the store. *Frank and Mae Sawyer* were selling provisions there as early as about 1916.

The Sawyers then moved to the South Portland Heights area and ran two different stores on Ocean Street. They returned to this corner in the early 1920s and continued to run a store here into the 1940s.

Frank and Mae Sawyer's house and store. This house once stood at the corner of Broadway and Evans Street, where Amato's is now located.

Courtesy of Dorothy Robinson

According to the Sawyers' niece, Dorothy Robinson, her Uncle Frank and Aunt Mae kept the store in the downstairs part and "Frank used to deliver meats," she says.

In the late 1940s and through the 1950s, **Cleon P. Hicks** ran the store. For a period of time in the 1960s and '70s, the site was home to service stations, including Kimball's Gulf Service Station and Ray-Mac Gulf. In the early 1980s, **Amato's Italian Sandwich Shop** opened at the site and continues in operation today.

The building at 1177 Broadway has hosted a variety of stores over the years. Mrs. Delia Moran operated **Moran's Store** in the 1920s, **Elmer Cash** ran a grocery in the 1930s, **Bartlett's Cash Market** was selling groceries, meats and fruit in the 1940s, and then it was **Allen's Cash Market** in the early 1950s through mid-1960s. **Vail's Variety** operated from the site in the late 1960s. Later retail stores included Debbie's Pet Boutique and Downeast Appliance. **A-Best Window** operated at this address until a fire damaged the building; the business then moved to its current location on the corner of Broadway and Lincoln Street.

The site at 15 Evans Street has seen its share of stores in recent years; since the 1970s we have seen *Stop-N-Go*, *Michael's Deli*, *A.J. Kennedy's*, and now *J.P. Thornton's*.

What would later become the South Portland Recreation building, the Goodwin's Market building on Nelson Road was situated roughly in front and to the side of where the South Portland Community Center now sits. The store carried a full line of groceries, a meat counter, and an extensive line of hardware supplies. Fred Goodwin, the store owner, is remembered fondly by many local residents.

Courtesy of Morley and Mildred Robinson

At 21 Nelson Road, *Goodwin's Red and White Market* was established during World War II, at a time when there was a boom in housing in the area. The incoming workers in the shipyards needed a place to live and, once the housing developments went up in this section of the city, Goodwin's was ready to fulfill the neighborhood's grocery needs.

Lu Schurman served as manager of the meat department at Goodwin's Red & White. Lu (left) is shown here with David Gutter who worked at the store as a meat cutter. Resident Marilyn Sherrard remembers shopping at the meat counter at Goodwin's Red & White. "Haddock was 59 cents a pound," she says.

Courtesy of Lucius Schurman

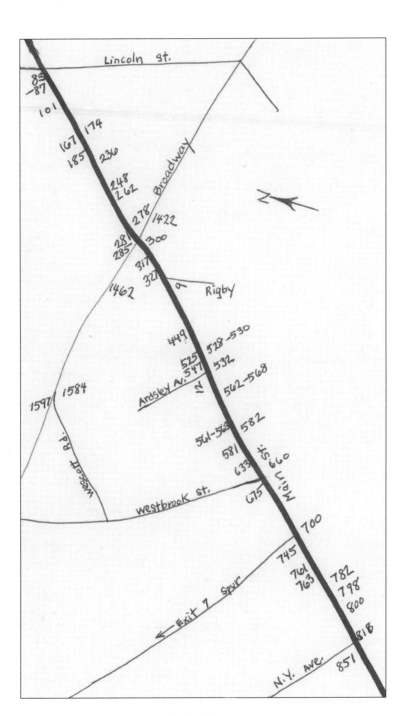

Main Street

Nine

Main Street and Vicinity

Ligonia, Cash Corner, Thornton Heights and Sunset Park, all neighborhoods along Main Street, saw significant changes throughout the 1900s. Originally, Main Street had much more of a "village center" feel in Thornton Heights with schools, groceries, bakeries and barber shops within walking distance of local residents. With the coming of the automobile, Route 1 became a very busy thruway and gas stations, motels and restaurants began to pop up along both sides of the street to service the increasing number of travelers.

During World War II, the activity along Main Street reached new heights with the constant flow of shipyard workers who lived south of the city all funneling through the area on their way to and from work.

The prosperous times of post-World War II meant increased traffic and travelers along Route 1. The Portland-to-Kittery section of the Maine Turnpike opened in December 1947. In the 1950s and '60s, places like the A&W Drive-In Restaurant and Howard Johnson's were in business, and then in the late 1960s and early '70s came places like Friendly's Ice Cream and Howdy Beefburgers along Main Street. After the construction of Interstate 295 in the early 1970s, travelers began bypassing the Thornton Heights area and business started moving into a period of decline. Although we still see a few restaurants and variety stores along Main Street today, it is only a fraction of the number of retail stores that existed in the 1940s through '60s.

Starting down in the Ligonia section of South Portland, there was a building with multiple addresses, 83-87 Main Street, near the intersection of Main and Lincoln Streets, roughly where the Trask-Decrow Machinery building now stands. The building had two apartments upstairs, and the first floor had another apartment plus a grocery store. *Aaron Katz* ran a grocery there in 1920. By the early 1920s, *Samuel Zolov* was running the store, then *Tabachnick & Ward* (Mae Tabachnick and Israel Ward, proprietors) in the mid-1920s and *Ligonia Cash Market* (Mae Tabachnick, proprietor) in the late 1920s.

Around 1934, *Fred Ganem Variety* opened in the 83-87 Main Street building, remaining in business until 1943. While Ganem's Variety was in business, around 1938, a lunchroom opened beside it. It was first known as *G & E Lunch*, run by George Ganem, then *Henry's Café* around 1939, run by Henry Alix, and finally *Hy-Way Lunch* around 1940-1942, run by Ernest Moulton.

Vincent's Grocery Store opened there around 1943 and was run by Pearl Vincent. According to Phyllis Ganem, Pearl and her husband Manuel lived in the apartment on the first floor next to the store. Manuel Vincent was a chef in Portland and left the running of the store to Pearl. She ran the store from the 1940s until around 1967.

Across from 100 Main Street where Locker Room Sports Cards & Memorabilia now stands, was a building at 101 Main Street. From about 1924 to 1927, Mrs. Jennie R. Bell ran a lunchroom; the business shut down, then reopened around 1929 as the **Bell Tea Room**, George H. Bell, prop., until about 1932. Around 1933, **Fred J. Ganem** ran a small general store from the site. Mrs. Jennie R. Bell then reopened a restaurant, running it from about 1934 to 1940. Around 1940, **Mrs. Shaw's Doughnut Shop** opened at 101 Main. Proprietor, Mrs. Celia Shaw, ran the business at 101 Main Street until around 1953.

Just up the street, **John Virgilio's Service Station** was in operation at 175 Main Street as early as the 1930s. In the late 1930s, he began running another service station at 167 Main Street. In July of 1941, Virgilio applied for a building permit to erect a "dine & dance" facility on the site.

The Rose Garden had booths and a dance floor inside. Locals remember it as the kind of place frequented by the younger crowd - a place to go for a beer and to meet a girl. Virgilio's Rose Garden and service station operated until the early 1950s; the two buildings were razed to make way for the construction of an access road to the new Veterans Memorial Bridge.

From the Collections of Maine Historical Society

Around 1949, the **Oxbow Snack Bar** was established by Conrad and Hazel Feroci at 174 Main Street. The couple then changed the operation to the **Oxbow Diner** around 1950-1951.

At 185 Main Street, **Fuller Bros.** was in operation in 1873 selling groceries and produce, run by Melville B. Fuller and his brother Vernal B. Fuller. Fuller Bros. operated into the late 1880s, when the name changed to **M.B. Fuller & Son.** Melville Fuller ran the business with his son Charles into the mid-1910s.

At 236 Main Street, **Myrtle Oldham Variety** was run out of a house around 1924. A florist business occupied the space over the rest of the 1920s and the 1930s. In the late 1930s and early 1940s, the building was mostly vacant, until **Pete's Grocery** operated in the late 1940s.

In the 1920s and 1930s, William E. Duddy was living at 248 Main Street and operating a harness shop at the site. **Handyman Rental Center** was established there by Merle Watson in 1954. When Merle Watson bought the house at 248 Main Street, he built the Handyman Rental Center right onto the house. In the photo (*below*), the roof of the original house can be seen behind the dinosaur. The house on the right in the picture was at 252 Main Street, between the Handyman building and what would later become One Stop Party Shoppe. The house in between was torn down.

Handyman Rental Center on Main Street   *Courtesy of the Merle Watson family*

Now site of **One Stop Party Shoppe**, 262 Main Street was a residence until the early 1960s. In the mid-1960s, **Howdy Beefburgers** opened. Howdy Beefburgers was part of a restaurant chain that had been started by the founder of Dunkin Donuts. The hamburger restaurant on Main Street ran until 1969 when it was destroyed by fire. The call came to the fire department around 2am.

A ruptured gas line fed the fire and fire fighters kept the fire under control until the gas company arrived; by the time the street was dug up and the gas shut off, the building was a total loss. The building was torn down and the site remained vacant for a few years.

Around 1973, another "hamburger joint" opened at 262 Main Street, **Carrolls Restaurant**. In the mid-1970s, Carrolls closed and the **Chowder Mug** operated from the site for about a year. In the late 1970s, the building was vacant. One last restaurant tried this location, the **Bar-B-Barn** in the early 1980s. That restaurant also closed fairly quickly. The **One Stop Party Shoppe**, which originated as the "Party Line" division of Handyman Rental Center with a showroom in the Handyman building, bought the building in the early 1980s, and remains there today.

In this 1960s photo, the Howdy Beefburger restaurant sign is on the left, and the restaurant itself is in the direct center.
Courtesy of the South Portland Historical Society

Andrew J. Cash, originally listed as a peddler in Ligonia in the 1870s and early 1880s, established **A.J. Cash Co.**, a grocery, in the mid 1880s at <u>278 Main Street</u>, situated at the junction of Main Street and Broadway. A.J. Cash Co. was a family business, with Andrew Cash, Jr. and Alphonso Cash working as clerks. Andrew Cash ran the business until about 1909, when Alphonso Cash took over the business.

Around 1916, **William A. Skinner** took over the grocery at 278 Main, and then **Maurice Troubh Variety** was at the site from the early-to-mid-1920s.

In the mid-1920s, 278 Main Street became a gas station and would continue as such under many different owners through the 1970s. The first gas station was a Mexican Petroleum station which operated into the early 1930s. The station then switched to American Oil and the "Amoco" sign hung for the rest of its existence. Some of the operators included Charles Lewis, Henry and Wesley Doughty, Brule & Buck, Clarence London, and McKenney's Amoco.

In the early 1980s, ***Village Food Stores*** operated for a few years, then ***Cash Corner Fish Market*** and ***Three Dory Fish Market***. In the late 1980s, Capitol Cash Register opened at this address.

Cash Corner, as seen in the 1920s and '30s. The sign on the gas station says "Pan-Am Gas". The house just to the left of the gas station is Hubert Hawker's house at 270 Main Street. His greenhouses appear to the right of the station. Hubert Hawker ran a florist business there from the mid-1910s to the mid-1950s. Courtesy of David Merrithew

Doughty's Service Station at 278 Main Street in the 1940s. Hubert Hawker's greenhouses can still be seen behind and to the right of the station.
Courtesy of the South Portland Historical Society

278 Main Street in the 1960s.

Courtesy of the South Portland Historical Society

Ward's Market at 281 Main Street was a general grocery store in Cash Corner, operating from the mid-1920s through the beginning of World War II. Prior to opening the grocery, the Ward brothers, James and William, ran a billiard and bowling operation from this address in the early 1920s. James Ward was also a barber, and when the two men opened *Ward Bros.* in the mid-1920s, the business was a combination grocery/barber shop.

By the early 1930s, James had left the business and William Ward changed the name to *Ward's Market.* Locals remember William Ward going by the nickname "Joe". Former resident Bob Dunlop remembers the wooden floor covered in sawdust; every night the sawdust would be swept up and a fresh layer put down to soak up any spills. "They always had a stalk of bananas hanging from the ceiling," say Dunlop. "There was a knife stuck in the stalk, you would pull it out and cut off a hand of bananas."

Along the back wall of the store was a meat case, on the left wall were canned goods, and on the right wall was a candy counter with penny candy. There were also cookies sold in bulk, in wooden boxes with glass covers. Cookies were scooped out and weighed. At night, according to resident Waverly Hammond, "He had a police dog he'd turn loose in the store and go home."

During World War II, George Ganem took over the site and started *George's Red & White Market.* Melville Perry took over the store operation around 1946 and renamed the store *Perry's Red & White Market.* Perry's closed by 1950.

In the vicinity of Rite Aid/Cash Corner today, the former Lano's Diner at 285 Main Street and the Red & White Market at 281 Main Street.

Courtesy of the South Portland Historical Society

One of the oldest stores in Cash Corner was at <u>285 Main Street</u>: **George W. Cash Store** and post office. Established around 1870, on the 1871 Atlas of Rural Cumberland County, George W. Cash was listed as a "dealer in dry goods, groceries, provisions, meal, flour, grain, boots, shoes, rubbers and general merchandise." By 1920, Harold E. Cash had taken over the store, which was called **G.W. Cash Company** at that time. At some point during the 1920s, Harold Cash changed the store's name to **Cash's Market**.

According to resident Waverly Hammond, Cash's Market was a store similar to Joe Ward's. They sold produce, canned goods and other groceries. Hammond remembers that Cash's would deliver groceries in an open truck, known as a "whippet". In the late 1930s, the store burned and Harold Cash built a new store at 327 Main Street.

In 1942, when the shipyards were taking over land in the Cushing's Point section of South Portland, George Ganem erected a platform at 285 Main Street and moved his diner from the shipyard area to Main Street. The diner opened as **Jimmy's Diner**. James Lano was listed as proprietor in 1942, George Ganem in 1943, and then Lawrence Arsenault in 1944-1946. By 1947, Arsenault had changed the name to **Larry's Diner**, but the name was changed to **Lano's Diner** when James Lano became proprietor again in 1948. Lano would operate his diner here for a few years, then had a new restaurant built across the street at 300 Main Street.

John Kapsemales opened the **Streamline Diner** at 285 Main Street in the early 1950s. It remained the Streamline Diner until Frank Venuti took over the restaurant in the early 1960s and renamed it **Frank's Diner**. The diner later became the *Cash Corner Diner* and was eventually moved in the 1980s to a location near Union Station in Portland.

Frank's Diner at 285 Main Street.
Courtesy of the South Portland Historical Society

Now the site of *Willow's Pizza & Restaurant*, 1422 Broadway had first been home to *Joe Manning's Store.* Established by Joseph Manning in the late 1920s, the store was originally located in a small wooden building. Former resident Bob Dunlop remembers that "the store had a big picture window with an ice cream table inside and two chairs with wire legs." Manning sold candy, ice cream, soda, Italian sandwiches, tobacco and very few groceries.

According to resident Waverly Hammond, Joe Manning also drove the Engine 5 fire truck. If a call came in, Joe would close the store and run next door to get the fire truck. Hammond remembers the store selling penny candy, canned goods and Italian sandwiches for 10 cents each. He also remembers the little square three-hole ice cream freezer inside.

Joe Manning ran the store from the late 1920s to the early 1940s. The store remained vacant through the rest of the 1940s, until Lumbe Lano opened *Lano's Variety* at the site, around 1950 (Lumbe and Jim Lano were brothers). Around the same time, the *Cash Corner Barber Shop* opened in a little building next door at 1418 Broadway.

Lano's Variety first operated from the small wooden building, then Lumbe and Sue Lano built the new building in front of the old one. According to Lumbe's wife, Sue, they sold milk, bread and grocery items, and made Italian sandwiches. Over time, they started making pizzas in the store, then began wholesaling frozen pizzas to Hannaford Bros and other small variety stores. Lano's Variety remained in operation until 1989, when *Willows Pizza & Restaurant* took over the business.

Lano's Restaurant at 300 Main Street *Author's collection*

After operating from the diner across the street, Jim Lano built ***Lano's Restaurant*** at 300 Main Street around 1950, on the former site of a gas station. After Lano's Restaurant closed in the mid-1970s, there were several other restaurants which operated from the building, including ***Cimino's Seafood Restaurant, Aladdin's Lamp, Peking Gardens*** and ***Mandarin House***. The building was later razed and a car dealership is now located on the property.

At 317 Main Street, ***Dairy Queen*** has served many generations of South Portland residents since it opened in the early 1950s.

After Harold Cash's market at 285 Main Street was lost in a fire, he built a new store at 327 Main Street. According to Alice and Bob Dunlop, ***Cash's Market*** was a small store, selling groceries, deli meats/cold cuts, beer and cigarettes. Cash's Market was in operation here from the late 1930s to the late 1940s, when Bob Collins bought the business and renamed the store ***Spot to Shop***. Spot to Shop operated until the early 1970s.

Bri's Variety was established here by Brian and Christine Dearborn around 1973. Starting out as a small variety store, the operation grew over the years to a full-scale restaurant with 21 seats on the first floor and another 58 seats upstairs. The restaurant was open at 5am daily and only closed for Christmas and a half day on Thanksgiving. Bri's Variety shut its doors on Dec. 31, 1997. The Stop & Shoppe Fuel Mart is now located at the site.

Courtesy of Peter and Paul Jeffery

George J. Ganem operated the **Broadway Market** out of a house at 1462 Broadway (close to Dairy Queen) in the late 1940s. The address was later utilized by the First National Bank of Portland.

In the mid-1920s, **Herbert Cash** ran a small grocery from the back of his house at 1584 Broadway. Located near the corner of Broadway and Wescott Street, the large house was opposite Dawson Street. According to resident Waverly Hammond, there was a driveway running the length of the house. Customers would go down the driveway and enter through a side door. The store was on the bottom floor of the house, virtually in the basement, as the two floors above were at a higher level.

Resident Waverly Hammond remembers the Moran's store being hauled in on a truck. The building was set in place at 1597 Broadway, across from Wescott Street, around 1938 and Mrs. Delia Moran ran **Moran's Store** (later called **Moran's Cash Market**) until the late 1950s (Mrs. Moran and her family had previously run a store at 1177 Broadway).

Fred Ganem took over the business in the late 1950s and changed the name of the market to **Freddie's Variety Store**. Fred Ganem had previously run a store at 101 Main Street. Freddie's operated from roughly 1958 to 1962. Around 1963, **Hatt's Cash Superette** was in operation, and then **Pooler's Variety** occupied the space from about 1964-1980. In the early 1980s, **Rick's Variety** operated for a year, then **Phil's Variety**. The store was vacant for a few years in the mid-1980s, then **Hungry's** was in business in the late 1980s.

This 1992 photo shows Folland's Variety, which opened at the end of the 1980s and ran until the mid-1990s. Mum's Variety was the last variety store to operate from this building at 1597 Broadway, around 1996/1997.
Courtesy of the City of South Portland

Prior to 1950, there were several diners and a variety store on Rigby Road, catering to the railroad workers. Some of the store operators in the 1910s and '20s include **Louis Piacitelli**, grocer, **Harry Peargtello**, grocer, **Rigmore Lunch, George F. Appleby Restaurant, Raffael Amadei Lunch** and **Rigby Lunch**. In the 1930s, **Larrabee Lunch, Arthur Cassidy Lunch, Rigby Diner** and **Charley's Diner** were in operation. In the 1940s, Edna Dearborn ran **Edna's Diner,** and that diner later became the **Terminal Diner**, run first by Martha Boucher, then by George Ganem around 1950.

At 9 Rigby Road, **Thomas C. Murphy** ran a variety store from the mid-1920s to early 1940s. He would then move his variety across to 12 Rigby in the mid-1940s. After Thomas Murphy's death in June 1948, his widow, Margaret continued operating the store until about 1950.

Caboose Lunch was established at 449 Main Street by Clarence Smith, a former yard conductor for the Portland Terminal Railroad Company. He ran the diner in the 1950s through early 1960s; his wife, Bertha Smith continued the operation into the early 1970s. According to Robby Ferrante, the diner originally ran 24 hours a day in the '50s and '60s, back when the Rigby railroad yard was bustling with activity.

Rudy Ferrante bought the diner in 1974 and renamed it **Rudy's Lunch.** His son Michael Ferrante bought the business around 1995 and renamed it **Rudy's All Star Diner** (Michael Ferrante had previously run the **All Star Deli** at the Maine Mall for about eight years prior to buying Rudy's Lunch). Around 1997, Michael Ferrante sold the business to Steve Cook. Cook has retained the Rudy's All Star Diner name and one of Rudy Ferrante's sons, Robby Ferrante, has worked at the diner since 1974, and still works there as of this printing.

Prior to the construction of the existing building at 525 Main Street, an auto service garage operated near that site, at 547 Main Street. The garage had several operators including Oscar Holman in the 1920s, **Hardison & Ramsey Auto Repairs** in the '30s and Lester Hardison's **Thornton Heights Garage** in the '40s and early '50s. According to resident Elford Messer, Ramsey's Garage had one pool table out back. "I used to like to play pool there," he says. It was also a fun place for kids, as the volunteer fire truck was kept in that garage. The building at 547 Main was removed in the mid-1950s.

In the early 1950s, the building at 525 Main Street was constructed and operated for many years as an IGA store. **Davis Super Market** was run there around 1951 by Paul Davis. Around 1952, the **Ezy-Way IGA Foodliner Super Market** was established. Joseph Smaha operated the business, and subsequently his son, Gerald Smaha, ran the business until 1965. (Gerald Smaha is the cousin of Tom Smaha, the owner of Legion Square Market).

The Ezy-Way IGA Foodliner underwent two expansions during its operation.
The above photo shows Jack Dempsey at the grand opening of the store's first
expansion.   *Courtesy of the South Portland Historical Society*

After the Smahas sold the business in 1965, the site remained an IGA store until roughly 1969. **Dollar Saver Market** operated from the site until 1971, and then Ted and Barbara Gill moved their **Gill's Pharmacy** into the space and renamed the business **Gill's Leader Drug**. After Ted Gill's death in July 1972, his wife Barbara continued the store operation until about 1976, when the business was sold to **LaVerdiere's Super Drug Store**.

Alice Smith Dunlop, a long time employee of Taylor's, Gill's and LaVerdiere's, remembers that Barbara Gill set up a boutique area in the store and hired a cosmetician. After LaVerdiere's took over, she says the boutique area was removed and replaced by aisles and shelving.

LaVerdiere's Super Drug Store at 525 Main Street.
Courtesy of the South Portland Historical Society

There were some other businesses which operated from 525 Main Street. Around 1974, Richard Flynn established *Flynn's Hardware*, which operated in the back of the building, behind Gill's. The entrance to Flynn's Hardware was on the left side of the building towards the back, facing the parking lot. Flynn's Hardware ran from the site until 1977 when they moved to 340 Main Street in Cash Corner.

Other building occupants over the years have included SNV Cleaners and Premiere Video. LaVerdiere's was later acquired by *Rite Aid Corporation*. The building has now been converted to a professional building with five separate companies operating from the space.

A variety of early businesses occupied the building at 528-530 Main Street, where *Deb's Sandwich Shop* is now located. In the storefront at 528 Main, *Watkins & Jordan Dry Goods Store* was in operation from around 1924 to 1926. Forest Watkins then left the business and *Harold E. Jordan Dry Goods Store* remained in operation until around 1928. The store was then taken over for a year, run as *Mrs. Flora M. Lamont Dry Goods Store*.

The store was converted to apartments for several years, before Atlas Baking Co. operated from the site in the late 1930s and early 1940s. *Capitol Grocery* opened around 1947 and was run by William and Samuel Hider until about 1960. The Hider brothers went on to run Hider's Variety at 372 Broadway.

Later businesses operating from the storefront at 528 Main include Jack's Barber Shop, World of Pets, and *Broderick's Sandwich Shop*.

The counter at Broderick's Sandwich Shop was very unique. There was a silver dollar about every four inches, each dollar accompanied by the signature and well wishes of various family, friends and original customers of Broderick's. There were over 200 silver dollars covering the countertop, which had a coat of varnish sealing in the coins and signatures.

Photo courtesy of the Broderick family

The **A&P** operated from 530 Main Street in the corner of that building from around 1924 to 1940. **Wakem's Cleaners** would take up residence in that storefront for over 30 years, from the 1950s through early 1980s. Later occupants included Hilltop Coins & Gifts, Baseball Bob's Card Shop, a television repair shop and now Posh! Hair Nails Skin.

Bennett's Ice Cream Bar   *Courtesy of Norma and Thomas Bennett, Jr,*

Bennett's Ice Cream Bar was established by Thomas and Helen Bennett in 1941. The shop was built on to the side of their house at 12 Ardsley Avenue, facing Main Street with a large parking lot in front. Bennett's Ice Cream Bar was a seasonal business, open from March to November. During World War II, before the Maine turnpike was built, buses carrying shipyard workers would stop at Bennett's so the workers could enjoy an ice cream cone before heading home. The Bennett's ran the business for over 30 years, serving homemade ice cream, sodas, pastries, and sandwiches. They were known for keeping a clean, immaculate store.

Thomas Bennett, shown here, was the brother of Stanley T. Bennett, who was the founder of Oakhurst Dairy. Thomas worked for Oakhurst for over 20 years before opening Bennett's Ice Cream Bar with his wife, Helen. He continued working part time for Oakhurst during the winter months, and "also enjoyed hunting and ice fishing," says his son, Tom. "His hobby was whittling, and his chickadees and seagulls were well known."

Courtesy of Norma and Thomas Bennett, Jr.

Inside Bennett's Ice Cream Bar, there was a juke box, with all the new songs of the day, and booth seating. For the most part, though, customers would come in and order their food and treats at the counter for take out.

Helen Bennett, shown here in front of the store, ran the store with her husband, Thomas. With the store attached to the house, they were always busy. Helen would bake pies, cakes, brownies and other custom-prepared foods for customers. She was known for her excellent marmalade, which would disappear soon after making it out onto the counter. "Helen's hobbies were rug braiding, crochet and needlepoint work," says her son, Tom.

Courtesy of Norma and Thomas Bennett, Jr.

One former employee, Alice Smith Dunlop, remembers how much everyone loved the Bennett's peach ice cream. "They had a big peach tree," says Dunlop, "and they would pick the peaches and make peach ice cream."

Helen and Thomas Bennett retired and sold their home/store in the 1970s. The building was later torn down and the site is now the location of Town & Country Federal Credit Union.

At 532 Main Street, across the street from Bennett's Ice Cream Bar, was *Cedric W. Brigham Variety*, popularly known as *Brigham's*. Brigham's was in operation from the early 1920s to the late 1950s and was much more than your typical variety of today. According to Alice Smith Dunlop, on the right side of the store was a soda fountain with bar stools, in the middle of the store there were three little marble tables with wire chairs, and on the left were glass cases with notions (needles, buttons, thread). On the back wall, Brigham's kept ammunition for sale. The store also sold hardware.

During World War II, the store was very conveniently located for those shipyard workers who lived south of the city. Sitting right on Route 1, Brigham's picked up a lot of business from workers stopping in to pick up some beer or a quick snack.

The building at 561 Main Street was originally home to several groceries, and when George Taylor's Pharmacy opened, the pharmacy was originally on the left side of the building at 563 Main, and the right side of the building (561 Main) remained a grocery for many years.

Some of the early groceries at 561 Main Street included the following: *William S. Libby,* about 1917-1918; *Katz & Co.,* around 1918; *Rufus L.*

Davis, around 1919; and *Fred W. Esty,* around 1920. According to J. Harold Higgins, his mother Mary Higgins was a widow and ran *Higgins Market* there around 1920. She carried cookies and pickles that came in barrels, and also sold canned goods and other groceries. She sold the business to William Johnson who ran *Johnson's Market* in the early to mid-1920s. *William Warner* ran a grocery at 561 Main in the mid-1920s.

Thornton Heights Market opened at 561 Main Street in the late 1920s. Claude Burnett ran the store in the 1930s and early 1940s; during that time, the store was also known as *Burnett's Market.* Burnett's Market was an IGA store. In the late 1940s, Paul A. Davis became proprietor and the store dropped the Burnett's moniker; it remained Thornton Heights Market until the early 1950s. *E. G. Shettleworth Co. 5 & 10¢ Store* was established by Earle G. Shettleworth in the early '50s. The store ran beside Taylor's Pharmacy until the early '60s. After it closed, Taylor's Pharmacy expanded into the space.

Pharmacist George E. Taylor started his *Taylor's Pharmacy* around 1924 at 563 Main Street. In addition to the prescriptions and drugstore items, the pharmacy also had a soda fountain and a post office.

In the above photograph of Taylor's Pharmacy, the automobile is parked on the side of the building facing Froswick Street. The mail box is on the front side of the building facing Main Street. The Thornton Heights Market can be seen on the right side of the building, 561 Main Street.

Courtesy of the South Portland Historical Society

John Edward "Ted" Gill began working for Taylor's in the early 1950s. By 1955, Ted Gill had taken over the pharmacy from George Taylor, but he kept the Taylor's Pharmacy name on the store. All of Gill's children helped out in the store, doing everything from dusting shelves to working at the counter and making Rx deliveries. Ted Gill's wife was a stay-at-home mom in the early years, but also performed bookkeeping and paperwork tasks (Barbara Gill would later go on to serve one term as a State Representative and seven terms as a State Senator).

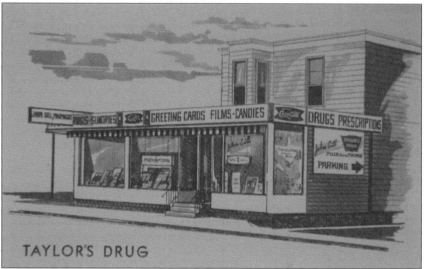

Taylor's Pharmacy.   *Courtesy of the South Portland Historical Society*

Gill's daughter, Karen remembers that for a few years, her father would give out ice cream cones to the neighborhood kids on the last day of school. "They lined up through the store and…some of the boys…tried to get in line more than once," she says.

In the early 1960s, the Gills increased the size of the store by remodeling and expanding into the space vacated by Shettleworth's next door. Alice Smith Dunlop, who was hired by Ted Gill in the mid-1960s and worked for Taylor's, Gill's and LaVerdiere's, remembers there was a wooden phone booth inside Taylor's Pharmacy. They sold items such as cosmetics, perfumes, greeting cards, boxed chocolates, candy bars, and cigarettes.

The store was destroyed by fire on March 31, 1969. Gill's daughter, Karen recalls, "The day the store burned down,…while it was on fire, a big guy, not an employee, grabbed the big old heavy cash register and carried it out of the store. I remember washing blackened pennies that night at home. They also tried to save most of the paper Rx files." Gill's daughter, Jo remembers, "Dad's friends, mostly all pharmacists, set up a make-shift pharmacy in a trailer within two days. Dad was beside himself…"

Firefighters on the scene of the Taylor's Pharmacy fire in 1969
Courtesy of the Gill family

As the pharmacy operated from the trailer, a new brick building was constructed on the same spot as the original pharmacy. It was completed and the pharmacy moved in by the end of 1969. At that time, the name was changed to **Gill's Pharmacy**. The pharmacy sold most of the same items as before, except that the soda fountain was not replaced.

In 1971, the Gills moved the pharmacy to 525 Main Street and changed the name to **Gill's Leader Drug**.

There are four storefronts in one building at 562-568 Main Street, which are now occupied by Jung's Quality Alterations (562 Main), Maine Institute of Tae Kwon Do (564-566 Main Street) and as of this printing, a vacant store at 568 Main.

At 562 Main, early grocers included **Clarence E. Goff** around 1925, **Standish Bradford,** around 1926, **Barnes Market** and **Whitmore's Market** in the late 1920s, **First National Stores** from the early 1930s to late 1940s, **Mac's Food Mart** around 1949-1950 and **Thornton Heights Market** in the early 1950s. The store then became **Fehlau's Hardware Center** from the early 1950s to the early 1960s. Around 1963, Frank Toppi opened **The Pizza House**, which then became **The Pizza Store** around 1964-1965. The storefront was vacant for a few years before **Langella's Pizza House** opened in the late 1960s, selling pizza, Italians and other sandwiches, chips and soda. Later stores included *Jimmy's Specialty Market, Langille's Variety, Main Street Market* and Home Plate Sports Cards.

At 564 Main, some of the early stores included *Frank Jones' Restaurant* around 1927, a pool hall in the early-to-mid-1930s and *Ottaviano Breggia Shoe Repair* in the late '30s to early '40s. *D & E Potato Chip Co.* was run by Dorothy Allan and Ernest Hasey around 1942-1943; they made kettle-cooked potato chips. *Fehlau's Hardware* would expand into the space at 564 Main while they were in operation in the 1950s and early 1960s. The space has alternatively been annexed to the 562 or 566 storefronts over the years; Maine Institute of Tae Kwon Do is currently occupying the 564-566 Main storefronts.

At 566 Main, early stores included *Frank Jones' Lunch* around 1926, then *Thornton Heights Bakery/Restaurant* in the late 1920s, operated by Frank Jones. *Barnes' Market* was in operation around 1931-1932; Barnes had previously operated at 562 Main. Other stores in the 1930s were *Chandler's Main Street Market, Tedford's Grocery and Restaurant*, and *Hy-Way Lunch*. George's Beauty Studio operated around 1940, then *Mrs. Wilma W. Roberts Bakery and Restaurant* in the early 1940s. Later stores included *Emery's Variety Store*, the Launder-In and Fancy That Beauty Boutique.

At 568 Main, after *Irving Hicks Barber* around 1926-1927 and *Kenneth Royal's Barber Shop* in the late 1920s and early '30s, Louis J. Nappi established *Nappi's Barber Shop* in the mid-1930s and continued in operation into the early 1970s. *The Cookie Jar Pastry Shop* occupied the space around 1976-1977 (now on Shore Road in Cape Elizabeth). That storefront later housed upholstery businesses and is vacant at the time of this printing.

Now site of Bishop & Company consignment shop, 581 Main Street was home to Friendly's Ice Cream Restaurant from the 1970s to the year 2000.
Courtesy of the City of South Portland

In the 1930s, Morton Price was running a gas station at 600 Main Street. Resident Elford Messer was a paper boy in those days. "I used to go there to pick up my papers…the filling station was open all night, we used to hang out there as kids…then they built a little mom and pop store," he says. That little mom and pop was located next door at 582 Main Street and was known as *Price's Store.* Price also added a lunchroom at one point. "They had a jukebox," says Messer. Messer also remembers the store as a place to buy a soda and a whoopie pie. The little variety store remained in operation into the 1960s; during its later years, it was run by Earl Price.

The *Snak-a-Roo Restaurant* was established at 633 Main Street around 1963 by Virginia Boyd. The restaurant closed down shortly thereafter, but reopened around 1966 as *Snak-a-Roo Ice Cream.* The ice cream stand was only open until about 1967, then closed and later became the site of *Dunkin Donuts*, which opened around 1970 and remains in operation today.

Clifford E. Cash ran a grocery at 660 Main Street from around 1912 to 1916; he had previously operated a grocery store at 753 Main Street from about 1908 to 1911. *Thornton Heights Market* took over the space at 660 Main around 1917, replaced by *Arthur C. Glazier Grocer* around 1918. Around 1920, *Charles L. Seavey Grocer* was in operation, then *Morris Cohen Grocer* from about 1922 to 1924. The store remained vacant for many years until *Mrs. Shaw's Doughnut Shop* opened in the late 1930s and continued into the mid-1940s. Later businesses at the site included a furniture repair company and TV repair shop. The site was used by Coca Cola for storage in the 1960s and early '70s. A parking lot now covers the property.

Although the restaurant building on the corner of Westbrook and Main Streets is vacant at the time of this printing, 675 Main Street was home to *Se-Lect Foods* restaurant in the late 1930s to early 1940s and *Howard Johnson's Restaurant*, which opened around 1942. Howard Johnson's was a summertime business in the early years, the kind of place that locals and travelers alike would frequent for ice cream, hot dogs, sandwiches, fried clams and great salt water taffy. The owners also ran a restaurant in Florida; when the restaurant closed here in the fall, some of the waitresses would head to the Florida restaurant to work during the winter months. After Howard Johnson's closed in the mid-1980s, the site was home to *Blackbeard's,* and then *Tony Roma's, A Place for Ribs* in the late 1980s and 1990s.

Home to a variety of businesses through the years, 700 Main Street was originally a house and dairy run by Charles R. Dean. Dean's *Cloverdale Dairy* started around 1920; Dean had a milk room on the property where he pasteurized and bottled milk. He ran the dairy for over three decades, and then built a motel on the property: the Gateway Motel.

Cloverdale Dairy at 700 Main Street.
From the antique post card collection of John and Patti Vierra, Gray, Maine

The Gateway Motel at 700 Main Street was open in the 1950s and '60s, run first by Charles Dean, later by Mauro Danforth. The photo above shows the Dean house still standing to the right of the motel.
Courtesy of the Maine Turnpike Authority

The Steer House Restaurant and Steer Inn Motor Lodge.
Courtesy of the Portland Press Herald

Construction of a new motor inn/restaurant facility began in the fall of 1967. In 1968, the **Steer Inn Motor Lodge** and the **Steer House Restaurant** opened.

After the Steer House operated for a few years, the **Stage Coach Inn and Restaurant** opened in the early 1970s and continued until around 1975. The **Yankee Squire Restaurant** operated for a short time around 1976; Tony Notis (who also ran the Bridgeway Restaurant in Knightville) was a partner in that restaurant. After a fire, the Merry Manor Inn opened around 1977 and the following year, **John Martin's Merry Manor Restaurant** began operation.

The inn has changed owners over the years, later becoming a Days Inn and then a Best Western. The Merry Manor Restaurant operated for over a decade, followed by several other restaurants, including **Friar Tuck's Restaurant**, **Jordan's Seafood Restaurant**, and now **Governor's Restaurant**.

Walter Tupper started a grocery at 745 Main Street around 1925. Around 1928, **Mrs. Eva C. Brackett** took over the store, and then around 1930, the store became **Pine Grocery Co.**, operated by Thomas DeGruchy and Jennie Richards until about 1934. The building is now a residence.

Edward Black moved **Black's Variety Store** from 763 Main Street to 761a Main Street around 1957. He continued operating the store into the late 1970s. The building is now a residence.

Around 1944, **The Hy-Way Store** opened at 763 Main Street. The store became **Ray's Market** around 1947 and then **Bubar's Market** around 1952. Bubar's Market continued until about 1955. Around 1956, Edward Black established **Black's Variety Store** at 763 Main. The following year, the business moved next door to 761a Main Street. The building at 763 Main Street is now a residence.

Antonio Esposito ran a grocery store at 782 Main Street from about 1944 to 1948. Around 1949, **Sunset Variety** was in operation. In the 1950s, **Darling's Lobster Pound** and later **Mack's Lobster Pound** were open in the summers. **Mitchell's Fruit & Produce** operated from around 1960 to 1965 and **Merriman's Fruit & Produce** was in operation around 1966. The building no longer exists.

Bananas and strawberries were for sale at Mitchell's Fruit & Produce at 782
Main Street. Blaine Motel can be seen in the background at 778 Main Street.
Courtesy of the City of South Portland

The A & W on Main Street in 1980.   Courtesy of the Portland Press Herald

The *A & W Drive-In Restaurant* opened at 798 Main Street in 1957. A
new restaurant was built in 1970 and the restaurant eventually closed in 1985.
Southside Plaza was constructed soon thereafter and Red Wing Shoes was one
of the first tenants. The *Portland Pie Company* is one of many businesses
now located at the plaza.

Lum's Restaurant at 818 Main Street.   *Courtesy of the City of South Portland*

At <u>818 Main Street</u>, **Lum's Restaurant** was built and opened for business around 1969. After operating for over a decade, Lum's shut down and **Donnelly's Restaurant** operated from the site until 1989. The **Wok Inn** bought the site in 1989.

Another business in the distance in the above photo is Robert Hall Clothes, which operated from <u>800 Main Street</u> from the 1960s to mid-1970s. That site is now home to **The Right Sub**.

The Maple Inn Dining Room and Filling Station   *Courtesy of Barbara Cook*

From the early 1930s until World War II, the **Maple Inn Lunchroom and Tourist Camps** was located at 851 Main Street, on the corner of Main Street and New York Avenue. The trolley tracks on Main Street can be seen in the photo on the previous page. After WWII, Tilton & Smith service station operated from the corner for a few years, followed by Roger & Gordon service station for a year.

In 1947, Stuart and Esther Brown began operation of **Stu Brown's Variety and Service Station**. According to Arline (Brown) O'Reilly, when her parents took over the business, the main building was one-story with an attic; there was also a lift outside, to the right of the building. The Browns added dormers to the building, creating a living space upstairs for themselves and their two children, and they built a garage to the right, enclosing the lift.

Stu Brown's Variety and Filling Station   *Courtesy of Arline Brown O'Reilly*

Stu Brown's offered the standard variety store fare; Esther made Italian sandwiches for customers in the kitchen on the first floor. Arline O'Reilly remembers how her mother just loved all of the kids: "She was always giving penny candy to the kids. They'd give her a penny and she'd always give them extra". O'Reilly also remembers her dad's political life: Stu Brown served on the South Portland City Council and also served in the 100th and 101st State Legislatures. Stu and Esther attended several Governor's Balls. The contrast was dramatic: "She pumped gas and danced with governors," O'Reilly says of her mother.

Esther Brown had a tremendous work ethic. The store was open virtually every day, year round, closing for only a half day on Christmas. She also had a heart of gold and, as many residents and her daughter warmly remember, was always there for anyone in need in the neighborhood.

Courtesy of Arline Brown O'Reilly

In the late 1960s, ***Foster's Variety and Service Station*** was in operation. Then from the early to late 1970s, Don Foshay ran ***Foshay's Corner Store***. Foshay's made Italians, meatballs and pizza. According to Don Foshay, the store

sponsored a basketball team in the Rec League over the years, and they also employed many South Portland High School students in the store.

For 20 years, Don Cook ran ***Cookie's Variety*** from that corner. ***Rolando's Redemption Center*** is now operating at the site.

Courtesy of Barbara Cook

Ten

Redbank/Maine Mall

While the Maine Mall is not exactly what one would call a "neighborhood store", the development of the area has been one of the major factors affecting the shopping habits of the residents of South Portland in recent years. In this chapter, we will take a brief look at Redbank and then wrap-up with a brief overview of the Maine Mall's history.

Redbank

The history of the Redbank stores is not a lengthy one. Prior to World War II, the land in that area was owned by Thomas Phinney, who operated a farm and dairy business. During the war, a government housing development was established at Redbank to alleviate the housing shortage for shipyard workers. After families began moving in in 1943, an immediate need for groceries and supplies developed, and stores soon followed.

One of the first stores to open was **Berry's Red & White Market** at 586 Westbrook Street, run by George Berry. After the war, the store became **Redbank Red & White,** and from about 1950 to 1963, the store operated as **Redbank Supermarket**. From about 1964 to 1968, John Robinson ran **Robinson's Market**. After H & H Laundromat ran from the site for a few years, Stan and Barbara Cress established **Stan's Market** and Stan's Laundromat in the early 1970s. In the late 1970s, Gordon and Gloria Libby took over the business and continued to run it as Stan's Market. Tim Davis bought the store in December 1986 and established **Tim's Variety** at the site. In the summer of 1987, Davis put in a take out window and operated a dairy bar from the building for a few years. Tim's Variety Store remains in business today.

Another store opened in the 1940s, **Your Handy Store** at 565 Westbrook Street. That store was run by Alfred Vigue into the early 1970s. Later stores at that address include **Foshay's Variety Store, Savoy's Variety Store, Mutt & Jeff Variety Store**, Bud's, **Broderick's Sandwich Shop**, and the Doctor's restaurant/bar.

At 555 Westbrook Street, Frances Stern operated **The Village Variety Store** up until the mid-1980s. The Village Variety continued in business into the late 1980s under different management. **Show Time Video** and B & D Cycles would later operate from the site.

Maine Mall

Former South Portland City Manager Bernal Allen was instrumental in the development of the Maine Mall. Back in 1965, the city owned about 40 acres of land near the intersection of Gorham and Payne Roads (later renamed Maine

Mall Road). Much of the land in the vicinity of the Maine Mall had been home to a pig farm. Allen convinced the Board of Industry to purchase another 150 acres to hold for the possible development of a large shopping center.

Bernal Allen had this sign erected near the intersection of Payne and Gorham Roads. Shown in this May 1967 photo, the sign reads: "So. Portland Industrial District, Sites Available, All Utilities Water Sewer Public Transportation Electric & Etc., Community Financing Available, Tel. 799-6652, Bernal B. Allen, City Mgr."   Courtesy of the City of South Portland

With all of this land available, Bernal Allen went to work enticing developers. By November 1967, Allen had hooked a Massachusetts developer, who chose this site to build a shopping center. By December of 1967, the developer had purchased the first 22 acres of an estimated 190 acres that would be built upon.

Jordan Marsh (now site of Macy's) was the first store to open, in August of 1969. The store measured 200,000 square feet and the Jordan Marsh Car Care Center was located in a separate building in the parking lot.

Clearing land for the construction of Jordan Marsh.
Courtesy of the City of South Portland

The Maine Mall officially opened in 1971 with close to 50 stores open for business. Some of those first stores included Sears, Gold Star IGA, F.W. Woolworth, Deering Ice Cream, Casual Corner, Owen Moore, Chess King, Thom McAn, Anderson-Little, Benoit's, Ward Brothers and York Steak House.

When the Maine Mall opened in 1971, the building was anchored on either end by Jordan Marsh and Sears. In this photo, the addition heading towards the food court and JC Penney had not yet been constructed. Service Merchandise is located in the building towards the top right. On the lower left, only one tower of the Sheraton has been constructed.

Courtesy of the Maine Mall

The "Jord" section of Jordan Marsh's sign is being lowered in this 1996 photo, in preparation for the Macy's signs to go up.

Courtesy of Peter and Paul Jeffery

The Lechmere store in 1998; now site of Best Buy
Courtesy of Peter and Paul Jeffery

This 1999 photo shows the Filene's Basement building. The building had previously been home to Value House and Service Merchandise. Present day occupants are Chuck E Cheese and Vinny T's of Boston Restaurant.
Courtesy of Peter and Paul Jeffery

This 1996 photo shows Crickets Restaurant on Philbrook Avenue. The building originally housed the Hu Ke Lau for many years. Sebago Brewing Company now occupies the space.
Courtesy of Peter and Paul Jeffery

Home Quarters at Clarks Pond in 1999, now site of Bob's Discount Furniture and Home Goods.

Courtesy of Peter and Paul Jeffery

Arby's (now Pizzeria Uno) can be seen in the foreground of this aerial photo of the Mallside Plaza. Shaw's Supermarket takes up the left half of the plaza, Bookland is just to the right of Shaw's.

Courtesy of the Maine Mall

The old Zayre store at Mallside Plaza. Zayre's was later replaced by Ames and is now site of Dick's Sporting Goods.

Courtesy of the Maine Mall

This 1996 photo shows the old Bed & Bath store, Herman's Sporting Goods and Bookland at the Mallside Plaza.

Courtesy of Peter and Paul Jeffery

This 1981 photo shows Marshall's and Heartland Food Warehouse near the airport. Staples and Burlington Coat Factory are now located at this site.

Courtesy of Peter and Paul Jeffery

In this photo from 2000, East Side Mario's had closed and 99 Restaurant and Pub was about to open. Many restaurants have come and gone from the Maine Mall area over the last 30 years.

Courtesy of Peter and Paul Jeffery

Retail shopping has undergone enormous change over the past hundred years. From the full-service grocers of the early 20th century with their flour and pickle barrels sitting on sawdust-covered floors, to the mass merchandisers of today, it is hard to imagine what the shopping habits of our grandchildren and great-grandchildren will be like in years to come.

When we look back at some of our beloved shopkeepers, the wonderful men and women who believed in hard work and caring for their customers, we see that they played a key part in our community. A nostalgic look at our stores in turn leads us to a nostalgic look at the way life once was. Where we shop, where we "hang out", is a reflection of how we live and how we interact with one another. May we pay tribute to our forebears by striving to play a key role in our community today!

Acknowledgements

It would take another volume to individually thank everyone who assisted me in the research and production of this book. To the hundreds of people who shared their time, their memories, their assistance, and in some cases, their precious family photographs, I am so grateful for your help.

There are some people who I would like to specifically thank who took considerable time and effort to assist me, and at times pointed me in the right direction to find an answer:

Sylvia Angell	Bob Dyke	Dan Lunt
Lee Bumsted	Mike and Linda Eastman	Herb Pray
Carol Campbell	Belle Graney	Craig Skelton
Doris Cook	Frank and Kay Greenlaw	Mason Philip Smith
Cathy Counts	Peter and Paul Jeffery	David Soule
Cori Curran	Rosella Loveitt	Mary Anne Wallace
Jim DiPhilippo	Ben Lunt	Parker Wells

I'd also like to thank the City of South Portland, the South Portland Historical Society and its directors, the South Portland Public Library (Marian Peterson, the library director, as well as Marie Chenevert and the rest of the fantastic library staff), Mark Thompson and the Portland Harbor Museum, the Maine Historical Society, the Portland Press Herald, and the librarians in the Portland Room at the Portland Public Library.

For their incredible gifts of time and support, thanks to Linda Eastman, Lisa Bathras Flocatoulas, Craig Furbush, Rachelle Parise, and Tyla Schaefer for acting as my editors, lending their feedback and suggestions.

Also a huge thanks to my parents, who encouraged me and who were always there for any help that was needed. Most especially for being there for their grandkids while I was off doing research!

And finally, my love and greatest thanks go to my husband, Ed for allowing me the time to pursue this endeavor, for understanding my desire to preserve this piece of history, and for supporting me along the way. My children also deserve the biggest thanks. Not just for being patient while their mom was working (what must have felt like *all the time*), but for using the time as an opportunity to learn how to write their own books. Josie, Jenny and Tommy, I am so proud of you and I know that you will all publish your own books one day. I love you!

Index to Businesses